'This book is important. Hel   r
approachability and her eng   ﹥
The Bible Doesn't Tell Me So is extremely helpful, both for Christians
who have been subjected to abuse and for those wanting a strong
biblical approach to addressing domestic abuse issues. It is both
theological and practical and offers an authoritative and ultimately
healing approach to scripture for women who have been abused.
I know it will make a positive difference to women's lives!'
Natalie Collins, gender justice expert and author of *Out of Control:*
Couples, conflict and the capacity for change

'I have all too often seen the Bible I love weaponised by men to control
and subordinate their wives. The sad truth is, domestic abuse is as
prevalent in the church as it is in the world outside. I am deeply grateful for this book and Helen's detailed study and balanced explanation
of the texts that have been used throughout the centuries to "bash"
women. It is an academically excellent book which sheds light on the
complex scriptures it covers, yet remains immensely readable. It is
thorough and profound, and it enables the reader to not just wrestle
with these verses, but also to consider God's original plan for the
relationship between men and women. This book shows the Bible is
liberating for women, challenging for some men and I pray *The Bible*
Doesn't Tell Me So will become a core text for leaders as they learn
to recognise and respond to domestic abuse within their churches.'
Bekah Legg, director of Restored

The Bible Reading Fellowship
15 The Chambers, Vineyard
Abingdon OX14 3FE
brf.org.uk

The Bible Reading Fellowship (BRF) is a Registered Charity (233280)

ISBN 978 0 85746 989 2
First published 2020
10 9 8 7 6 5 4 3 2 1 0
All rights reserved

Acknowledgements
Unless otherwise stated, scripture quotations are taken from The Holy Bible, New International Version (Anglicised edition) copyright © 1979, 1984, 2011 by Biblica. Used by permission of Hodder & Stoughton Publishers, a Hachette UK company. All rights reserved. 'NIV' is a registered trademark of Biblica. UK trademark number 1448790.

Scripture quotations marked NRSV are taken from The New Revised Standard Version of the Bible, Anglicised edition, copyright © 1989, 1995 by the Division of Christian Education of the National Council of the Churches of Christ in the United States of America. Used by permission. All rights reserved.

The safety plan (p. 166) is reproduced from Natalie Collins, *Out of Control: Couples, conflict and the capacity for change* (SPCK, 2019), pp. 270–73, with kind permission of the publisher and the author.

Every effort has been made to trace and contact copyright owners for material used in this resource. We apologise for any inadvertent omissions or errors, and would ask those concerned to contact us so that full acknowledgement can be made in the future.

A catalogue record for this book is available from the British Library

Printed and bound by CPI Group (UK) Ltd, Croydon CR0 4YY

THE BIBLE DOESN'T TELL ME SO

WHY YOU DON'T HAVE TO SUBMIT TO DOMESTIC ABUSE AND COERCIVE CONTROL

HELEN PAYNTER

Contents

Acknowledgements and dedication 6

Preface 8

Introduction 12

I THE WEAPONISATION OF SCRIPTURE

1 A wife's proper place 26

2 The subordination of women 54

3 Divorce 68

4 Forgiveness and suffering... 77

5 When pastor turns predator 88

II THE TRUTH WILL SET YOU FREE

6 God is for the oppressed 100

7 Jesus: fellow sufferer and non-toxic man.................... 113

8 You are of immense value... 127

9 Silenced and hidden no more 140

III THREE PERSONAL ADDRESSES

10 To those trapped by an abuser.................................... 150

11 To church leaders 152

12 To the perpetrator 160

Taking it further... 163

Notes.. 170

Acknowledgements and dedication

One name appears on the front of this book, but don't be fooled – producing a book is a team sport, not a solo one, and this would never have appeared without the input, support, expertise and assistance of many individuals, for whom and to whom I am exceedingly thankful.

I am grateful to the expert staff at BRF, especially Olivia, Karen, Eley and Daniele, who believed in this book and have enthusiastically helped it to come to fruition. They are not just publishers of a manuscript; they are passionate advocates of what I am attempting to achieve here – so much so that at the height of the Covid-19 crisis they actively sought out the extra work of pre-releasing a chapter with a view to helping women who were locked in with an abuser. Thank you all, it has been a delight to work with you once again.

The work certainly wouldn't have been completed without the enthusiastic support of my family. Much of it was written in the early mornings of our 2019 summer holiday, and my husband's first actions on waking each day were to seize upon and read the new chapter. I am ever grateful for his sharp eye on my writing; his is always my first and most loving editor's pen.

I am, in fact, acutely thankful for the two principal men in my life – my husband Stephen and my father Bruce – for being the epitome of non-violent, non-abusive, non-toxic men. I have known nothing but support and love from you both, and I thank God for you. Nor can I fail to mention the wonderful women in my life who have loved and supported me: my much-missed mother Eleanor, who would have been so proud to see this book published, and the feisty, determined and compassionate women that I am privileged to call my daughters, Susanna, Louisa and Victoria. May you always know your value and dignity and may you be blessed with partners who honour and love you as Christ loves the church.

I'm also hugely grateful to those who read the manuscript at various stages in its preparation: Katy Adams, Natalie Collins, Kym Hildyard, David Batchelor and F. Each of you brought your own experience, perspective and expertise to bear upon it. The book is much the better for your comments and suggestions.

Most of all, this book could not have been written without the many women, survivors of domestic abuse, who spoke with me as I prepared to write. I am grateful beyond words for your willingness to relive and share painful and private memories, and for entrusting me with your stories. I have been moved and humbled by your courage, your tenacity, your love and your faith. I contemplated trying to name you all using initials only, but I feared forgetting someone. (Some of the 'interviews' were spontaneous conversations in churches and coffee shops.) But then I remembered the book of Lamentations, much of which is written in the voice of an abused woman. Each chapter is structured as an acrostic, with a verse for each letter of the Hebrew alphabet. It is as if the woman is saying, 'This is the A to Z of my pain – let nothing be omitted.' So here is the A to Z of my gratitude. You know who you are. Thank you from the bottom of my heart. This book is for you.

Written in worship of the Lord Jesus, the ultimate non-toxic man, and the only truly complete human.

Preface

We start with a story from a very long time ago.

A downtrodden woman from an abusive domestic situation sees – beyond all hope – the fulfilment of her heart's desire. Something she has longed for and prayed for over a very long time has come about. In response, she begins singing a song of worship.

> My heart rejoices in the Lord…
> My mouth boasts over my enemies,
>   for I delight in your deliverance.

But then her song takes a surprising turn. First she addresses her erstwhile abuser:

> Do not keep talking so proudly
>   or let your mouth speak such arrogance,
> for the Lord is a God who knows,
>   and by him deeds are weighed.

Then she turns her attention more widely. Everything is being turned on its head:

> The bows of the warriors are broken,
>   but those who stumbled are armed with strength.
> Those who were full hire themselves out for food,
>   but those who were hungry are hungry no more.
> She who was barren has borne seven children,
>   but she who has had many sons pines away.
> The Lord brings death and makes alive;
>   he brings down to the grave and raises up.

The Lord sends poverty and wealth;
    he humbles and he exalts.
He raises the poor from the dust
    and lifts the needy from the ash heap;
he seats them with princes
    and makes them inherit a throne of honour.

How can she speak so boldly about these great themes of reversal? Because she knows the character and power of God.

For the foundations of the earth are the Lord's;
    on them he has set the world…
It is not by strength that one prevails;
    those who oppose the Lord will be broken.
The Most High will thunder from heaven;
    the Lord will judge the ends of the earth.
1 SAMUEL 2:1–10

You may recognise the song and be familiar with the story behind it. The woman is Hannah, one of two wives of a man named Elkanah. The abuse she has been subjected to is the mockery and disdain of the other wife, because Hannah was childless.

You could describe this story as one of the hinges of the Bible. Hannah is singing because she has had a son. The son is Samuel, and he is going to change world history.

* * *

The Bible has another hinge, even more significant than the birth of Samuel the kingmaker. It, too, is heralded by a childless woman – in fact, two childless women – giving birth. And Mary (for the two women are Mary, mother of Jesus, and Elizabeth, mother of John the Baptist) sings for wonder and joy, just as Hannah did. In a resounding echo of Hannah's song from so many generations before, Mary anticipates a great reversal for rich and poor, proud and humble.

My soul glorifies the Lord...
He has performed mighty deeds with his arm;
    he has scattered those who are proud in their inmost
        thoughts.
He has brought down rulers from their thrones
    but has lifted up the humble.
He has filled the hungry with good things
    but has sent the rich away empty.

LUKE 1:46, 51–53

When I was preparing to write this book, I had a striking conversation with someone who had been subjected to abuse by a church leader. She made reference to a blog post I had written, where I had used the phrase 'reading the Bible to hear the voice of God'.

'It was wonderful to read those words,' she told me, 'because for so long, whenever I have opened my Bible, all I have been able to hear is the voice of my abuser.'

And this is why I begin with Hannah and Mary, with these two brave women who found their place in the great plans of God. These are strong women who formed the turning points of the biblical narrative. These are prophetic women, who could see with the eyes of faith the plan the Father is working on: the elevation of the downtrodden and the toppling of the mighty.

Was it Mary who first taught Jesus the words of Isaiah the prophet? For it is just this theme that Jesus chooses when he makes his great pronouncement in Nazareth at the beginning of his ministry:

The Spirit of the Lord is on me,
    because he has anointed me
    to proclaim good news to the poor.
He has sent me to proclaim freedom for the prisoners
    and recovery of sight for the blind,

> to set the oppressed free,
>> to proclaim the year of the Lord's favour.
> LUKE 4:18–19

And just a little while later, in his famous sermon on the plain, he emphasises the same thing:

> Blessed are you who are poor,
>> for yours is the kingdom of God.
> Blessed are you who hunger now,
>> for you will be satisfied.
> Blessed are you who weep now,
>> for you will laugh…
> But woe to you who are rich,
>> for you have already received your comfort.
> Woe to you who are well fed now,
>> for you will go hungry.
> Woe to you who laugh now,
>> for you will mourn and weep.
> LUKE 6:20–26

* * *

The Bible does not belong to abusers. And though you may hear echoes of their voices there occasionally, they are only found there to be contradicted, subverted and humbled.

The Bible was written for people like you.

Introduction

In February 2019, I received an email from someone I had never met. We'll call her Jenny. Jenny had heard me speaking on a series of podcasts produced by Bible Society, talking about some of the stories of sexually violent men in the Old Testament.[1] As a result, she contacted me to tell me something of her story and to ask me some questions.

Jenny has been married for decades to a man who for a long time served as a lay preacher with a major denomination in the UK. During their marriage he consistently emotionally abused her, undermining her confidence and self-worth. He also physically abused her, sexually abused her and raped her.

Jenny is now living apart from her husband, although they are still married. She is gradually healing, in body and soul. But she had some major questions, and many of these centred around what the Bible says to people like her. With her permission I quote from her email:

> I would like to understand what happened. How could a Christian marriage end like this?
> What does God think of it?
> What was the church doing?
> I know the Bible very well – we read a chapter aloud each night for 38 years, so I know all the hard parts.
> I know that Hagar escaped and God sent her back. Why?
> I know that the Levite abandoned his concubine to save a man and she died at the hands of men. Who cares?
> I know it says wives should keep silent in church and ask their husbands at home. Huh!
> If you can make any sense of all this and help the churches to do so, I shall be glad.

The issue for Jenny was particularly acute because for her, married to a preacher, scripture had been interpreted to her *by her husband* for decades. He had told her many times that Esther was an exemplary wife, a model of beauty and availability. Each time he said it, it made her feel more unattractive, more ashamed. He told her, again and again, that her role as a wife was to obey him. When she didn't, she was being a terrible wife. Or so he said.

Jenny knew her Bible well, but because of the way her husband had interpreted it to her, she could now only find in it themes which appeared to validate his treatment of her. Scripture had been *weaponised* against her. It had been shaped into something that could only hurt, not heal.

* * *

Jenny's email arrived in my inbox at just the right moment. As founding director of the brand-new Centre for the Study of Bible and Violence at Bristol Baptist College, I had been starting to think about the ways that the Bible speaks into situations of modern violence. I had also been starting to investigate ways in which the Bible is being used to endorse violence. When Jenny's message arrived, we began an email correspondence and then met in person. She helped me to see that there would be value in a book that debunks some of the dreadful ways that the Bible has been used by abusers. I hope I helped her to see that the use of the Bible in this way is an appalling distortion of God's word.

Since then I have done a lot of research, speaking with survivors of domestic abuse and coercive control, and also with those who work with them, through personal friendship or in a professional capacity. I offer this book as the fruit of that research, brought into dialogue with my study of the scriptures.

* * *

At this stage we should probably offer a definition of domestic abuse and coercive control. As well as physical hurting and sexual coercion, abuse can take a number of other forms, including emotional manipulation, bullying and financial control. The UK government website has a helpful checklist, which I reproduce below.[2] Notice that your partner does not have to physically hurt you for your relationship to be abusive.

If you answer yes to any of the following questions, you might be in an abusive relationship.

Emotional abuse
Does your partner ever:
- belittle you, or put you down?
- blame you for the abuse or arguments?
- deny that abuse is happening, or play it down?
- isolate you from your family and friends?
- stop you going to college or work?
- make unreasonable demands for your attention?
- accuse you of flirting or having affairs?
- tell you what to wear, who to see, where to go and what to think?
- control your money, or not give you enough to buy food or other essential things?

Threats and intimidation
Does your partner ever:
- threaten to hurt or kill you?
- destroy things that belong to you?
- stand over you, invade your personal space?
- threaten to kill themselves or the children?
- read your emails, texts or letters?
- harass or follow you?

Physical abuse

The person abusing you may hurt you in a number of ways.
Does your partner ever:

- slap, hit or punch you?
- push or shove you?
- bite or kick you?
- burn you?
- choke you or hold you down?
- throw things?

Sexual abuse

Sexual abuse can happen to anyone, whether they're male or
female. Does your partner ever:

- touch you in a way you don't want to be touched?
- make unwanted sexual demands?
- hurt you during sex?
- pressure you to have unsafe sex – for example, not using
  a condom?
- pressure you to have sex?
- If your partner has sex with you when you don't want to,
  this is rape.

Have you ever felt afraid of your partner?
Have you ever changed your behaviour because you're afraid of
what your partner might do?

* * *

It won't surprise readers of this book, I guess, that there are domestic
abusers within church. But it does surprise many in the churches. In
fact, rates of abuse perpetration within church are about the same as
rates in the general population.[3] It's just that it's often brushed under
the carpet, overlooked or smoothed away. People put their 'church
faces' on and pretend that all is well.

Churches ought to be safe places for people who are abused to come and find solace, help and restoration. Sadly, the situation is often the exact opposite, because the abuse of scripture to manipulate a woman into tolerating harm is not confined to abusers. Perhaps with the best of intentions and often in entirely well-meaning ways, churches sometimes use the Bible to make the situation *worse* for the woman, when she plucks up the courage finally to disclose her situation.

Women I have spoken with describe how the church has told them it is their duty to win their husbands back by their meekness and compliant spirit (using 1 Peter 3:1–2). Or that because their husband has not been sexually unfaithful, she has no biblical grounds for divorce (using Malachi 2:16 and Matthew 5:32). Or that it is their Christian duty to forgive (and that forgiveness means allowing him to continue to abuse her and any children they have).

As I say, often the people giving advice in this way are trying their best to live faithfully and to mend a marriage. But they are frequently doing more harm than good.

* * *

There is another way in which the Bible can be brought to play where someone is abusing their partner. This is where the culture of the church provides the right conditions for abusers to develop and flourish. When this happens, the abusers may not even need to use the Bible at home. The church culture already appears to support what they are doing.

I have heard stories like this as I have interviewed those who have been subjected to abuse by a partner. Representative quotations would be as follows:

- The church taught me a passive way of being a Christian woman.
- We were taught that women should be meek and stay in the background.
- There was no framework or mechanism that would enable me to complain or raise concerns.
- There was such an emphasis on sin and guilt that I felt continually dirty and ashamed.
- I knew that divorce wasn't an option. Once you've made your bed, you have to lie in it.
- I was groomed for abuse, and the church played a part in that grooming.

Let's just let that last quotation linger in our minds for a moment: 'I was groomed, and the church played a part in that.'

Of course, the church wasn't *trying* to do that. It wasn't *aiming* to set itself up in such a way that women felt crushed, worthless and useless. It wasn't *intending* to establish a culture of male dominance that would give an abuser permission to cause harm.

But that is what happened. That is what many of the women I spoke with have had to contend with. The Bible was used in a way that established a church culture of male dominance and female subservience. And women were groomed to endure abuse.

God forgive us.

* * *

The Bible can be made to say just about anything, if it is taken out of context. It can be made to say that the earth stands on pillars (1 Samuel 2:8, NRSV), that certain men should castrate themselves (Galatians 5:12) or that we need to fetch Paul's cloak and scrolls from Troas (2 Timothy 4:13). In actual fact, of course, it is saying none of those things to us. Here we have examples of imagery, rhetoric and comments made about particular situations. We need to read carefully, to think about what the writer is saying in the larger context and to piece together what that means for us.

A good minister will help train their congregation to do this well. She or he will encourage their congregation to learn to interpret scripture for themselves, while always valuing the insight of those who have studied the Bible long and hard. Sadly, and for a variety of reasons, people in the churches are sometimes not equipped to handle the Bible well.

And an abuser will not open up interpretive possibilities. He will shut them down. He will not invite discussion about context and interpretation. He will tell you what the Bible means and use it to beat you with. He may genuinely believe what he is saying, or he may be deliberately manipulating it. But what he is doing is using the Bible to control, to oppress, to harm. He is weaponising the Bible.

But the Bible does not support the abuse of anyone. It can only appear to do so if it is manipulated and twisted.

* * *

So what I am writing here is the book I wish Jenny had had 20 years ago. It is for all the Jennies who are still out there, being told that the Bible says they must tolerate the intolerable.

As I write this book, I have four types of reader in mind.

First, I am writing to women who are being subjected to domestic abuse or coercive control within a Christian setting, and who have scripture weaponised against them by the abuser or by their church. We are going to take a good hard look at the passages that abusers and churches use and investigate whether or not the Bible really is telling you that you have to endure your abuse. Spoiler alert – it isn't!

What I'm not suggesting is that you take any of the things we look at and use them to contradict your abuser. Often this will be unsafe. Only you can decide whether that is likely to be helpful or to put you at risk of further harm.

The person I most want to persuade is *you*.

There are many things arrayed against you, as someone with an abusive husband. He has probably whittled away your self-worth and self-confidence. He may have threatened to take your children away or hurt you. You may be concerned about the financial implications of leaving. You may be feeling a sense of guilt and shame (we'll talk about this in chapter 8). You may have tried to tell friends, or your minister, and found they have ignored or disbelieved you.

You may also be feeling confused and conflicted. Perhaps you are wondering why things are so difficult. Perhaps you are wondering if it is somehow your fault. Maybe you aren't even sure if what you are experiencing really amounts to abuse.

I'm sorry that there are so many things stacked up to make it hard for you to find safety and freedom. But please know this: the Bible is not one of them. The Bible is on *your* side.

It is my fervent hope and prayer that you will read this book and find it helpful. But first, **make sure you're safe**. Is it safe to take this book to your house? Do you need to disguise it somehow? Do you need to leave it in the home of a trusted friend? Don't let reading it put you in danger.

* * *

Second, I am writing to people who are supporting women being abused. You might be friends with someone who needs to read this book. It may be that she isn't ready to read it yet, but you might be able to discuss the ideas with her.

This won't be the only book you need to help your friend effectively. It's not a how-to guide for those who are supporting women in abusive situations. There are some excellent books like that around, and I suggest some of these at the end.

What's distinctive about this book is that it is intended to help your friend understand that God is on her side. That God is not – whatever she may have been told – demanding that she put up with it. That it is fine to leave her partner – to divorce him, even. That she should prioritise her own safety and the safety of any children involved.

* * *

Third, I'm writing to church leaders.

Friends, I'm a local church minister myself. I know that you have many calls on your time and many priorities. I wish I didn't have to press another one on you.

But domestic abuse and coercive control are common in churches. If you have a congregation above about 30 people, then it is more likely than not that someone in your church is experiencing it.

That means they are experiencing, or are at risk of, misery, suffering, danger and long-term trauma.

Tragically, churches have sometimes been complicit in abuse. They have made it harder for women to get out of abusive marriages. They have tried to fix things that are beyond their expertise and deal with matters that should have been referred to the police.

You and I might differ on some things. You might be the leader of a church that has traditional gender roles; I'm a female minister. But even if we do disagree on this, I believe this book is important, and I urge you to take it seriously, because I take the Bible very seriously indeed. Whatever our beliefs about women's roles in church, I'm sure we agree that they should *never* be subject to abuse in the home. I will speak to you directly in chapter 11 and try to offer some final comments about using the Bible to build churches that are supportive of those who have been subjected to abuse.

So, church leaders, please read this book. Please make sure that you and your church are equipped to be part of the answer, not part of the problem. Please seek justice for those in your congregation, just as you do for those charities that your church supports. It is surely a core outworking of the gospel.

* * *

And finally, it is just possible that some abusers will choose to read the book. If that is you – welcome! I will address you directly in chapter 12, but please don't skip over chapters 1 to 9.

* * *

Many readers will already have noticed the gendered language that I am using here and will continue to use throughout the book. Let me explain why I have made this decision.

In the UK, cis and trans men and women are subjected to domestic abuse. Abuse is perpetrated in heterosexual and gay and lesbian relationships. I understand this. Nonetheless, the vast majority of abusers are male, and the vast majority of people who report abuse are female. The most up-to-date statistics from the Crown Prosecution Service show this:

2018–19 UK domestic abuse prosecution statistics
- 78,624 defendants were prosecuted. 92% of them were male.
- 81,035 complainants were recorded. Where the sex of the complainant was recorded, 82.5% of them were female.

CPS Violence against Women and Girls Report 2018–19, p. A13

And if we consider coercive control, which has been a criminal offence in the UK since 29 December 2015, this is almost exclusively a male against female crime.[4] 17,069 offences of coercive control were recorded in the year ending March 2018.[5]

But this alone would not justify my using female language for victims and male language for perpetrators. My reason for doing so is because I am specifically addressing *the use of the Bible* in situations of domestic abuse. And, as far as I can tell, the Bible is being used by husbands who abuse wives, not the other way around.

Likewise, I have chosen to use the language of husband and wife rather than partner, even though I am aware that domestic abuse is perpetrated within civil partnerships, cohabiting relationships and other forms of domestic set-up. My reason, again, is because in households where the Bible is viewed as authoritative, couples are usually heterosexual and married. I realise that this is a generalisation, so forgive me if you are an exception to this. I don't intend to exclude anyone.

One final comment about the language I have chosen to use. I understand that many people object to the language of 'victim', and I have tried to minimise it in favour of 'survivor' or some other expression. Sometimes, though, the 'victim' word is really the only one that will do. So, I honour those of you who have come out of the abuse strong and whole; I don't know how you have managed it, and it moves me every time I hear such a story. And I also honour those of you who continue to live with brokenness, within a relationship or outside it. I do not seek to victimise you, but it is important to acknowledge that what has been done to you is utterly, utterly wrong.

* * *

So let me finish this introductory chapter by explaining how the rest of the book is structured. It is split into three parts. In the first part, we will consider some of the falsehoods – misunderstandings and outright lies – that are used by abusers or churches to prevent women from getting free from the abuser. I group these together under the broad title 'The weaponisation of scripture'. We will look at each one in turn and seek to understand it properly.

Then we will look at some more positive things that the Bible has to say to women and victims of violence. I find it interesting that in the days of American slavery, the masters were pretty careful about which passages they allowed their slaves to read. What are the passages that the abuser doesn't want you to read? Let's crack them open and let the light flood out!

And then, third, I have three chapters that directly address three of the types of people who might be reading the book. As I have said, it is mainly aimed at women whose husbands are currently abusing them – or who were previously subjected to abuse. I will therefore conclude my message to you in chapter 10 by providing some possible ways forward. I will point you to other things you might read and signpost you to people who are willing to listen and help you. Chapter 11 addresses church leaders, and chapter 12 any perpetrators who are reading this book.

* * *

Let me say, finally, that as a minister and a teacher of the Bible, I take the responsibility of the interpretation of the Bible very seriously. I do not believe that we can twist it and bend it to suit our purpose. Nor can we throw out the bits we don't like. So in this book we will look carefully, honestly and thoughtfully at the texts that have caused problems. But you won't hear me say that the Bible is a terrible, patriarchal, abusive thing. I love the Bible and believe it is God's word. I also believe that it is liberating. Let's explore how.

I

THE WEAPONISATION OF SCRIPTURE

1

A wife's proper place

I kept the table. I was the mop-and-bucket brigade. I was there to make him look good.

Ex-wife of a minister who abused her

In this chapter we will look at the way that certain scriptures have been weaponised against wives. These include the misinterpretation of some parts of the epistles and the misapplication of certain Old Testament examples. We will look at them in turn.

'Wives, submit to your husbands': an abuser's charter?

There are three places in the Bible where we read this instruction, worded in one way or another: Ephesians, Colossians and 1 Peter. There is also a section in 1 Corinthians where Paul speaks about male headship. If the abuser is using scripture, there is a good chance he is using one of these passages. And, on the face of it, they look pretty stark.

But there's quite a bit to be said about them and about what they might actually be saying to us today. We will focus on Ephesians.[6]

Ephesians 5:21–33 – who is to submit?

Wives, submit yourselves to your own husbands as you do to the Lord.

EPHESIANS 5:22

First, take a look to see where the paragraph break in Ephesians 5 occurs in your Bible. Does it fall after verse 21 or before it?

The paragraph breaks are not indicated in the original text. They, along with the chapter breaks and even the verse breaks, have been added later in an attempt to be helpful. This is also true of the little headings that go at the beginning of sections – these have been added by the translators. They are not part of the Bible.

Often these breaks are very useful to the reader. Imagine, for example, trying to find your way around the book of Isaiah without any verses, paragraphs or chapters marked. That's 66 chapters of unbroken text! (That is what Jesus would have had to do in the synagogue in Nazareth; see Luke 4.)

But sometimes the people who made the decisions got them wrong. They may have misunderstood the flow of the argument. And sometimes the decisions reflected their unconscious presuppositions – their bias.

Compare the 1984 version of the NIV with the 2011 version, for example. I've kept the section headings in.

NIV 1984:
[21] Submit to one another out of reverence for Christ.

Wives and Husbands
[22] Wives, submit to your husbands as to the Lord…

NIV 2011:
Instructions for Christian Households
[21] Submit to one another out of reverence for Christ.
[22] Wives, submit yourselves to your own husbands as you do to the Lord…

The assumption made by the editors of the 1984 version is that the instruction for mutual submission belongs with the verses before it, which particularly relate to the church. But the 2011 editors have concluded that it is better to place it with the instructions for husbands and wives.

So, who is right?

Well, verse 21 quite likely serves as a 'hinge' in the text – a little sentence that can equally apply to both situations. But if we have to put it on one side or the other of the section break, it is better to place it after the break. There are several reasons for this, but the strongest is that there is actually no verb in verse 22 – it is implied by the previous verse. Translated very literally, it reads:

[21] Submit yourselves to one another out of reverence for Christ.
[22] Wives, to your own husbands as you do to the Lord.

Separating these two verses makes literal nonsense out of the second one.

But what matters is that the best way to read the instruction for wives to submit to their husbands is immediately after the instruction for all believers to submit to one another. The call for people within the church to prefer each other's needs is common in the letters. Consider these other words of Paul, for example, addressed to the whole church:

Serve one another humbly in love.
GALATIANS 5:13

Do nothing out of selfish ambition or vain conceit. Rather, in humility value others above yourselves, not looking to your own interests but each of you to the interests of the others.
PHILIPPIANS 2:3–4

Before Paul asks wives to do anything, he first asks all disciples to be mutually submissive.

* * *

There's another helpful point that looking hard at the original text can show us. Here I need to get a bit technical, but not for long.

You may know that English verbs can be active or passive. Most verbs we use are active:

- I *hit* the ball.
- She *sings* a song.
- They *will read* the book.

We could say all of these things with a passive verb instead, though it sounds rather clumsy:

- The ball *was hit* by me.
- The song *is sung* by her.
- The book *will be read* by them.

Greek also has active and passive verbs, but it has a third category, too. This is sometimes called the 'middle voice'. This is often used when the person acting is doing it in relation to themselves somehow:

- At the trial of Jesus, Peter was *warming himself* by the fire (Mark 14:54).
- Herod *clothed himself* with royal clothing (Acts 12:21).
- The centurion sent word to Jesus not to *trouble himself* (Luke 7:6).

The word translated 'submit' in Ephesians 5:21 is in the middle voice. So a close translation would probably be 'submit yourselves to one another'.[7]

To submit oneself is a voluntary act. Nobody is causing you to submit; you are causing yourself to do it. There is an element of willing decision about it. Submission is not being imposed, but urged. (In other words, this is a million miles away from – for example – the coercive culture depicted in Margaret Atwood's *The Handmaid's Tale*.) Biblical scholar Ben Witherington puts it like this:

> 'Wives submit yourselves…' Paul does not tell the husbands to subordinate their wives or to exhort their wives to be subordinate. The exhortation goes directly to the wife.[8]

* * *

The abuser might be conveniently overlooking the fact that this instruction is part of a larger one about conduct in marriage. But don't let him fool you. In fact, far more is said to husbands than to wives. It might help to visualise it like in the table opposite, where instructions to husbands are on the left and to wives on the right. Comments that apply to both span both columns.

Let's look at the instructions to men and women separately.

Instructions to men

I don't know if you've ever visited a Roman city or town and explored the remains. I've been fortunate enough to see Roman remains in a number of places. I haven't been to Ephesus, but maps of the ancient city confirm that it fits the pattern – Roman towns always had public bath houses.

Having a bath in Roman times was an extended activity to occupy a wealthy man's leisure hours. After arriving at the bath house, he might first enjoy a wrestling match or have a philosophical discussion with a friend, before progressing through the elaborate sequence of rooms. As he moved through the bath house, each room got progressively hotter (with perhaps a cold plunge at the end). He would apply oil to his body and use a curved implement called a strigil to scrape it off,

Instructions to husbands and wives in Ephesians 5:21–33

Instruction to husbands	Instruction to wives
Submit to one another out of reverence for Christ.	
	Wives, submit yourselves to your own husbands as you do to the Lord.
For the husband is the head of the wife as Christ is the head of the church, his body, of which he is the Saviour.	
	Now as the church submits to Christ, so also wives should submit to their husbands in everything.
Husbands, love your wives, just as Christ loved the church and gave himself up for her to make her holy, cleansing her by the washing with water through the word,	
and to present her to himself as a radiant church, without stain or wrinkle or any other blemish, but holy and blameless.	
In this same way, husbands ought to love their wives as their own bodies. He who loves his wife loves himself. After all, no one ever hated their own body, but they feed and care for their body,	
just as Christ does the church – for we are members of his body. 'For this reason a man will leave his father and mother and be united to his wife, and the two will become one flesh.' This is a profound mystery – but I am talking about Christ and the church.	
However, each one of you also must love his wife as he loves himself,	
	and the wife must respect her husband.

along with dead skin cells. Or, more likely, he might get a slave to do it. He might get a massage. The bath house itself would be elaborately decorated, with mosaics on the floor, perhaps a courtyard with a colonnade to sit in the shade. There might even be an attached library or theatre. Clearly taking a bath was a very big deal.

Now listen again to what Paul says to husbands:

> Husbands ought to love their wives as their own bodies. He who
> loves his wife loves himself. After all, no one ever hated their
> own body, but they feed and care for their body.
> EPHESIANS 5:28–29

Male preening also goes on today, as the range of creams and grooming products on display in the high street testifies. And we also care
for our own bodies when we feed them, when we exercise them and
when we undergo health investigations or receive medical treatment.

Of course, people vary in how much care they take of their bodies.
But I think Paul's instructions here are pretty clear. In a town where
visits to the bath house were a frequent and indulgent way of life,
husbands should care for their wives as much as they care for their
own bodies.

In actual fact, the instruction is much more intense than this:

> Husbands, love your wives, just as Christ loved the church and
> gave himself up for her.
> EPHESIANS 5:25

How did Christ love the church? By laying aside privilege, by self-
giving, by going beyond all reasonable expectation to prefer the needs
of the other. In other words, by love that is spoken, lived out and
sustained; love that is non-coercive. As Paul puts it, in speaking of
Christ Jesus:

> Being in very nature God,
>   [he] did not consider equality with God something to be used
>   to his own advantage;
> rather, he made himself nothing
>   by taking the very nature of a servant,
>   being made in human likeness.

And being found in appearance as a man,
  he humbled himself
  by becoming obedient to death – even death on a cross!
PHILIPPIANS 2:6–8

When I preach on this passage, I sometimes speak of it as 'How low can you go?' Because Christ makes a sequence of downward movements: from being equal with God to taking human form, from human form to death, and not just any death but the very worst, most shameful death.

How's that for setting aside privilege, status and honour?

Husbands, love your wives like that, says Paul.

As Ruth Tucker says, 'If anyone squirmed in the pew of the first-century church, it surely must have been the husband, not the wife.'[9]

Instructions to women
But what about the instruction to wives to submit?

Wives, submit yourselves to your own husbands as you do to the Lord.
EPHESIANS 5:22

But Christ was a perfect man. He laid down his privilege, status and honour; he demonstrated love in every word and action. Submitting to a husband like that might be one thing; submitting to an abusive husband is another matter altogether.

There is something worth pointing out before we go any further. We should notice that little word 'own': 'Submit to your *own* husbands.' This is not a general command for (all) women to be subservient to (all) men. We will return to this theme in the next chapter.

Broadly, there are two ways of interpreting this instruction. I'm going to set them both out to you, because what you have been taught in church will almost certainly fall into one or the other category. And – here's the key thing – *neither* supports domestic abuse.

The egalitarian position
First, there are those who say that the instruction to submit was an instruction for its own time. Let me give you an example.

I'm a bit of a chilly soul. For about eight months of the year (though I guess climate change might alter this), I sit in the evenings with a throw over my legs. And I'm rather sensitive to draughts. So when my children come in and out of the lounge in the evenings, October to May, I'm usually heard to shout, 'Keep the door closed!'

Is that instruction a permanent one or for its own time? It's clear that it is an instruction for its own time. If it were a permanent command, then we'd have to find some creative ways of getting in and out of the room. And, to be honest, in June and July I'm often delighted to have the door open to get a through-draught. But, at particular times (such as in the winter when my daughters stand in the doorway chatting and the front door is open), the instruction is very much in force. Keep the door closed!

There are certainly instructions in the letters that fall into this category. We referred in the introduction to Paul asking for his cloak to be brought from Troas. Clearly, he is not asking us to do that – and nor is God. It was an instruction to Timothy.

I would argue that other things in the letters fall into this category, too – women covering their heads, for example. Rather than drag-and-drop instructions from the ancient Greco-Roman culture into the 21st century, we need to discover the underlying principle that Paul is applying and work out how that applies to us. (This isn't treating the Bible lightly, incidentally; it is taking it seriously enough to think very carefully about what it means.)

So, is the instruction to wives to submit one of these instructions that relates to its own culture? Maybe.

We know that all the letters are what are called 'occasional' documents. This means that the apostles wrote them for specific purposes or occasions – to guide the church in matters it was struggling with, to offer a corrective steer and so on. When we read the epistles, we are eavesdropping on an ancient conversation and wondering how it relates to us.

So, when Paul says, 'Wives, submit to your husbands', what is he thinking? There seem to have been some threats to marriage in the Ephesus church.[10]

First, it looks likely that the Christians there were inclined to think of marriage as they used to before their conversion – as a civil contract rather than a binding covenant. Paul wants them to understand that Christian marriage is something that represents our relationship to God, not just a common or garden variety agreement that can be annulled when one party has become bored. So, he shows how marriage is a mystery that points to the relationship between Christ and the church.

Second, there may well have been threats to marriage through immorality. Paul has certainly hinted at that several times in the letter (4:19; 5:3–6, 12, 18). If this is what he has in mind, then, once again, pointing to the uniqueness of this relationship and its similarities to our position with God is a helpful way of elevating it in his readers' minds.

Third, there were various movements in the early church which shunned marriage, perhaps through excessive zeal or because they thought that Jesus would be coming back any day (see Colossians 2:16–23 and 1 Timothy 4:1–3, for example). For such Christians, Paul may well be seeking to elevate the importance of marriage.

In order that marriage might indeed be seen as good and honouring to God, Paul needs marriage to be orderly. It needs to comply with what constitutes a good marriage by the light of the time. But in fact, Paul goes well beyond that.

There were two main strands of culture in the background of Paul's thought and the experience of the Ephesians.

The first was the Greco-Roman world. The Greek writer Plutarch had a great deal to say about marriage, for example. In his book *Moralia*, he sets out how he believes a well-ordered marriage should look:

> A virtuous woman ought to be most visible in her husband's company, and to stay in the house and hide herself when he is away.
>
> The wife ought to have no feeling of her own, but she should join with her husband in seriousness and sportiveness and in soberness and laughter.
>
> A wife ought not to make friends of her own, but to enjoy her husband's friends in common with him.
>
> Control ought to be exercised by the man over the woman, not as the owner has control over a piece of property, but, as the soul colonises the body, by entering into her feelings and being knit to her through goodwill. As, therefore, it is possible to exercise care over the body without being a slave to its pleasures and desires, so it is possible to govern a wife, and at the same time to delight and gratify her.

You can probably see points in common with Paul's words in Ephesians 5, but I hope you can also see some striking differences.

The second culture is the Jewish background of many of the believers and of Paul himself. There were many strands of Judaism in those days, and they didn't agree on everything. Nonetheless, many observed the oral law (the one that Jesus criticised the Pharisees for their preoccupation with), which was later written down as the Mishnah. Here is a flavour of what the Mishnah says about the rights and duties of wives:

> For all purposes is she in the domain of the father, until she enters the domain of the husband through marriage.

> Even if she brought him a hundred slave girls, he forces her to work in wool, for idleness leads to unchastity.

> She who rebels against her husband, they deduct from her marriage contract seven [half-shekels] a week... Until her entire marriage contract [has been voided].

> What a wife finds and the fruit of her labour go to her husband. And as to what comes to her as an inheritance, he has use of the return while she is alive.

> And those women go forth without the payment of the marriage contract at all [i.e. can be divorced without penalty]: she feeds him food which has not been tithed, or has sexual relations with him while she is menstruating, or she does not cut off her dough offering, or she vows and does not carry out her vow; she goes out with her hair flowing loose, or she spins in the marketplace, or she talks with just anybody. Also: if she curses his parents in his presence. Also: if she is a loudmouth. What is a loudmouth? When she talks in her own house, her neighbours can hear her voice.

> [If] there were blemishes on her while she was yet in her father's house, the husband has to bring proof that before she was betrothed these blemishes were on her body, so that his purchase was a purchase made in error.

[If goods or property] came to her after she was betrothed...
she may not sell them. Since [the husband-to-be] has acquired
possession of the woman, shall he not acquire possession of
the property?[11]

Again, I hope you can see some striking differences between this and
the words of Paul.

This is the background that Paul is speaking into. In this context,
his instructions to wives to submit are entirely unsurprising: that
is what good wives do (both Jew and Greek would have agreed).
But Paul's instructions for husbands and wives to submit to one
another as fellow believers is astonishing. And his instructions for
husbands to love their wives *like Christ loves the church* – that is utterly
revolutionary.

* * *

So, we might view Paul's words to couples as being astonishingly
countercultural, but not quite as countercultural as we might hope
in the 21st century.

We have two options when we read a law, an instruction or a piece
of advice in the Bible. This applies whether it is in the Old or New
Testament.

Option one is to lift it 'as is' out of its original context and apply it
today. You can probably see immediately that this would cause all
sorts of problems. We might end up stoning each other, for example.

The other is to notice how that law, instruction or piece of advice was
improving the ethics of the day; how it was helping to move society
towards what we might consider an ultimately perfect world. If we
notice this, then our job is to work out how we can move onwards
even further.

We may have, as a society, already moved a long way in this direction. Our job, then, is not to go backwards, but to move forwards still.

Perhaps a diagram might help. This is adapted from a book by William Webb called *Slaves, Women and Homosexuals*.[12]

Ancient culture ⟶ Bible ⟶ Our culture ⟶ Ultimate ethic

In other words, what the Bible urges was a good step in the right direction. But it was not the final step. We need to pay attention not to where the Bible has arrived at, but to the direction it is moving in – what it is saying to the society it is addressing. (We can often see this where Jesus moves things on from the Old Testament.)

Might this help us to understand Paul's words to husbands and wives? Perhaps. Compared to the way that women were viewed in the Greco-Roman world and in parts of Jewish society, the idea that husbands should love their wives while wives submit to them is an enormous leap forward. But it is – perhaps – not the final word on the subject. Perhaps the next step forward along the same trajectory is mutual love with equal power.

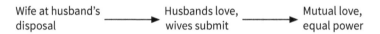

Wife at husband's disposal ⟶ Husbands love, wives submit ⟶ Mutual love, equal power

A possible example of power being shared equally between spouses is found in an odd place: the unsettling story of Ananias and Sapphira in Acts 5. You may recall the story: as new converts to the church, they had sold some property (a voluntary action) and given part of the proceeds to the apostles, pretending that they had given the whole sum. Peter questions Ananias, who lies about the matter and consequently drops dead. It is three hours later that his wife Sapphira comes in. As Ruth Tucker points out, Sapphira is held to be equally culpable and suffers the same fate:

There is no 'submission clause' that gets Sapphira off the hook. There was no recognized chain of command. That her husband was in authority over her wasn't worth a hill of beans when she was standing before Peter and the other apostles – and before the court of God's justice.[13]

There is one more thing that is worth saying. There is plenty of evidence in documents from the Greco-Roman world that slaves were badly treated: beaten and so on. If wives were routinely treated like that, we might expect to find a similar wealth of evidence saying so. But it isn't there. Some men must have been violent, human nature being what it is. But it does not appear to have been routine. So Paul probably wasn't thinking about this when he told wives to submit. He wasn't telling wives to put up with physical abuse.

The complementarian position

But there is another possible interpretation of 'wives, submit', and we need to consider this one, too. This is the opinion that Paul's instruction for wives to submit has enduring authority.

The argument generally is that Paul's comments relate to two deep underlying theological truths, one that began at creation and another that is in play now that the church has been established. As George Knight says:

With the words *submit to* and *head*, the apostle states the basic roles of wives and husbands respectively. God established those roles at creation, and they have as their analogue the roles of Christ and His church. Thus Paul can urge this special relationship of wife and husband because God in creation established it and Christ in his redeeming love to the church models and substantiates it for the redeemed community. W.J. Larking puts this consideration adeptly when he says that 'the instruction for conduct in marriage in Ephesians 5:22–33 becomes unquestionably binding when seen as a reflection of Christ's relation to the church'.[14]

As you may have guessed from my comments above, I am less sympathetic to this position, which is why I allowed one of the scholars who holds it to express it in his own words. But here's the thing: even in this position, less 'liberating' for women as it may be, a husband abusing his wife is utterly beyond the bounds of permitted behaviour.

May I repeat myself?

Whatever our theological opinion about wives submitting, a husband abusing his wife is utterly beyond the bounds of permitted behaviour.

In 1988 a group of conservative theologians released what is known as the Danvers Statement about biblical manhood and womanhood. It says many things that I do not agree with, in ways which go beyond the scope of this book. However, the paragraph which I quote here clearly affirms that abuse perpetrated within the home is a distortion of God's purpose, and I celebrate this:

> The Fall introduced distortions into the relationships between men and women. In the home, the husband's loving, humble headship tends to be replaced by domination…

In other words, even if one believes that wives should submit to the headship of the husband, this is intended by God to be within a mutually loving, supportive and affirming relationship. At its best, marriage should point us to our relationship with Christ. But when it goes wrong, the illustration breaks down.

* * *

There is perhaps one more thing to suggest, which I believe should emerge from this line of reasoning. Unfortunately it is not stated clearly as often as I would wish. This is the relevance of the little phrase 'as the Lord'.

> Wives, submit yourselves to your own husbands as you do to the Lord.
> EPHESIANS 5:22

To my mind, this has two edges. When a husband persistently fails to reflect the Lord in his words, his attitudes and his actions, his wife is released from her duty of submission. If he does not resemble the Lord, she need not submit to him as to the Lord.

So, for example, imagine that a man tells his wife to do something highly illegal – conceal a murder weapon, for example. Almost everyone would agree that this woman's responsibility to submit is here trumped by her responsibility to obey the law of the land and to cooperate with the investigation of a serious crime. Now let's imagine that the husband gives his wife an instruction to stand still while he beats her. Should she submit to him while he conducts *that* serious crime?

What if the instruction is not physically abusive but coercive? What if he forces her to manipulate her mother into giving him financial gifts; to lie to friends; to send the children to bed without food for a second day in a row? Should she submit to him in this? No: if her husband is not resembling the Lord, she need not submit to him as to the Lord.

* * *

We have considered the contentious passage in Ephesians in considerable detail. You will probably be pleased to learn that we will cover the relevant parts of 1 Corinthians and 1 Peter more briefly.

1 Corinthians 11

> I want you to realise that the head of every man is Christ, and the head of the woman is man, and the head of Christ is God. Every man who prays or prophesies with his head covered dishonours his head. But every woman who prays or prophesies with her head uncovered dishonours her head – it is the same as having her head shaved. For if a woman does not cover her head, she might as well have her hair cut off; but if it is a disgrace for a woman to have her hair cut off or her head shaved, then she should cover her head.
>
> A man ought not to cover his head, since he is the image and glory of God; but woman is the glory of man. For man did not come from woman, but woman from man; neither was man created for woman, but woman for man. It is for this reason that a woman ought to have authority over her own head, because of the angels. Nevertheless, in the Lord woman is not independent of man, nor is man independent of woman. For as woman came from man, so also man is born of woman. But everything comes from God.
>
> Judge for yourselves: is it proper for a woman to pray to God with her head uncovered? Does not the very nature of things teach you that if a man has long hair, it is a disgrace to him, but that if a woman has long hair, it is her glory? For long hair is given to her as a covering. If anyone wants to be contentious about this, we have no other practice – nor do the churches of God.
>
> 1 CORINTHIANS 11:3–16

This is one of the more difficult parts of Paul to understand – and that is saying something! It's not just modern writers who are perplexed by this passage. The great theologians of the early church Augustine of Hippo (354–430) and John Chrysostom (349–407) struggled with it.

In her excellent book *Rediscovering Scripture's Vision for Women*, Lucy Peppiatt carefully examines the possible interpretations, and I invite readers who would like to investigate this question in more detail to read her work. Part of the issue hangs on the meaning of the word translated 'head'. Sometimes it means 'authority' and sometimes 'source' (as in the head of a river). And there are other shades of possible meaning, too. This immediately introduces an ambiguity.

It is also unclear whether the passage is referring to husbands and wives or to men and women (the Greek words can be used for both meanings). And what does it mean to say that man is the glory of God but woman is the glory of man (v. 7)? There are many opinions on the matter.

One thing that can help us is to notice that Paul, in the Corinthian letters, often quotes *their* letter to *him*. Because there are no punctuation marks in the original script, we sometimes fail to notice that he has slipped into quotation mode. See, for example, 1 Corinthians 1:12; 6:12–13; 7:1; 10:23.

For this reason, and because Paul's argument is so interrupted by verses 7–9, Peppiatt concludes that they are the Corinthians' ideas that Paul is correcting, rather than Paul's instructions to them.

What we can say is this. The verse can be interpreted to mean either that there is an authoritative hierarchy between the man and the woman or that there is not. To a large extent the interpretation that we arrive at here will be influenced by the interpretation we have made of other key biblical passages (including those still to be discussed in this chapter and Galatians 3:28).

But we must take care, for an over-hierarchical interpretation of this text lends itself to male autocracy. As Ruth Tucker says:

> If the husband is the head – the ruler – in the home, who regulates him? Who determines if his headship is actually comparable to the headship of Christ? The husband himself? Is he alone the interpreter of the biblical standard? Is he the judge and jury in his own court case? Is he the referee, the umpire, in

his own ball game? Is he absolutely unbiased? Who determines exactly what male headship entails in each situation? Is there a written or unwritten standard for twenty-first-century domestic situations? At what point, if ever, does his behaviour make his headship invalid? Indeed, what are the consequences when husbands fail to live up to this standard?[15]

It is also worth pointing out, to return to Ephesians 5 for a moment, that Paul there only refers to male headship when he is speaking to women. He does *not* encourage the men to assert this over their wives.

1 Peter 3:1–7

Wives, in the same way submit yourselves to your own husbands so that, if any of them do not believe the word, they may be won over without words by the behaviour of their wives, when they see the purity and reverence of your lives. Your beauty should not come from outward adornment, such as elaborate hairstyles and the wearing of gold jewellery or fine clothes. Rather, it should be that of your inner self, the unfading beauty of a gentle and quiet spirit, which is of great worth in God's sight. For this is the way the holy women of the past who put their hope in God used to adorn themselves. They submitted themselves to their own husbands, like Sarah, who obeyed Abraham and called him her lord. You are her daughters if you do what is right and do not give way to fear.

Husbands, in the same way be considerate as you live with your wives, and treat them with respect as the weaker partner and as heirs with you of the gracious gift of life, so that nothing will hinder your prayers.

1 PETER 3:1–7

This is perhaps the hardest passage of all the ones that I need to deal with in this book. But we have laid a bit of the essential groundwork in the section above, so I am able to make my remarks more briefly.

As in the Ephesians passage, wives are instructed to submit *themselves* (v. 1), using the middle voice. As we saw, this implies that they are being asked to submit from voluntary agency rather than in forced submission. And, again as in Ephesians, wives are told to submit to their *own* husbands; the relationship between a husband and wife has a particular character that does not exist between women and men generally.

Also, we should recall that although in the ancient world wives were viewed as subordinate beings who should be subservient to their husbands, violence against them was the exception not the rule. They are not, here or in Paul's letters, being told to submit to violent men.

Now we need to look at the particular situation that Peter[16] is addressing, because it is not the same as the situation Paul is addressing in Ephesians and Colossians. In those letters it is believing husbands who are being referred to. But here, it is a more mixed audience. Peter is speaking to Christian women whose husbands may or may not also be believers:

> If any of them do not believe the word, they may be won over.
> v. 1

Society at the time expected wives to conform to their husband's religion. The writer Plutarch, whom we quoted earlier, made that clear:

> It is becoming for a wife to worship and to know only the gods that her husband believes in.

So the Christian wife of an unbelieving husband was in a difficult position. This is probably why Peter tells them not to submit to fear (v. 6). How are they to try to navigate the difficulty? By being brave and testifying clearly to their husbands. Most of all, by being a good wife – according to the way 'good wives' were viewed in the day.

As my friend Steve Carter, who is an expert on 1 Peter, writes:

The letter encourages wives not to fear intimidation by their husbands… but it does not tell them to endure beatings.[17]

But the letter also addresses believing husbands. We don't get the 'love' word here – different author, different emphasis. But what we do get is a very surprising and overlooked little sentence.

Husbands, in the same way, show consideration for your wives in your life together… so that nothing may hinder your prayers.
v. 7 (NRSV)

In other words, if you want your prayers answered, men, respect your wives! And if God turns his back on inconsiderate husbands, how much more will he upon abusive ones?

* * *

There is one element of the argument in 1 Peter which we haven't addressed so far, which concerns the reference to Sarah as an exemplary wife (v. 6). This leads us on to the broader idea, often put about by abusers, that certain relationships in the Bible are to be viewed as models for modern marriage. We will look at these now.

'Ideal' wives in the Bible

As far as I can tell, these stories are used by abusers in one of three ways. These might vary in exact details, but they typically go something like this:

- Abraham treated his wife badly in the Bible, so it's alright for me to.
- Sarah was an ideal wife, and you need to be like her. If you aren't, it's alright for me to hurt you, because you deserve it.
- Esther was an ideal wife. Why aren't you as beautiful and compliant as her? I'll use that story to humiliate you.

There is an excellent answer to this. It's one that the abuser won't tell you, of course: **there isn't a single marriage in the Bible which is viewed as ideal.** That's because, of course, there is only one person in the Bible who acts in a morally perfect way, and he wasn't married.

Let's look at some of the more commonly used examples.

Sarah

Sarah is perhaps our toughest case to answer, because she is held up by Peter as an example of an obedient wife:

> This is the way the holy women of the past who put their hope in God used to adorn themselves. They submitted themselves to their own husbands, like Sarah, who obeyed Abraham and called him her lord.
>
> 1 PETER 3:5–6

But Peter doesn't say that she was perfect. Nor does he say that her husband's behaviour was exemplary. Let's list some of their faults.

Abraham *twice* pretended that Sarah was his sister in order to protect his own skin. And he is clearly criticised for doing so (Genesis 12:18–19; 20:8–18). The second time, the action was particularly dreadful because he had just been told that his promised son would be born through Sarah (17:19). In other words, Abraham was negligent towards both the promise of God and the safety of his wife. **This behaviour was *not* okay, and the Bible does not suggest it was okay.**

Sarah is portrayed as quite a nasty piece of work, too. It was she who told Abraham to rape his maidservant Hagar. Interestingly, in the early Greek version of the story (which our New Testament writer would have been using), Abraham is said to 'obey' Sarah at this point (16:2). Sarah then treated the pregnant girl so badly that she ran away (16:5–6). Later, Sarah again treated Hagar badly and had Abraham send her and her son into the desert (21:8–10).

And at the point when Sarah calls Abraham 'lord' or 'master', she is being disrespectful to him – questioning his potency, even:

> Sarah laughed to herself as she thought, 'After I am worn out and my lord is old, will I now have this pleasure?'
> GENESIS 18:12

In fact, Sarah is so dominant in these passages that one commentator believes that Peter had his tongue at least partly in his cheek!

> The use of Sarah as an example of obedience shows that Peter was not devoid of a sense of humor. In Genesis, Abraham is shown as obeying Sarah as often as Sarah obeyed Abraham.[18]

I suspect that this is overstating the case, but it does highlight for us the importance of not being over-simplistic when we read these words in 1 Peter. Sarah may have been a good wife in the main, but she certainly wasn't a model of compliant wifely obedience! If Peter is saying, 'Be like Sarah', he cannot possibly be demanding utter subservience. To me, the standout element in the relationship between the two characters is Abraham's grief after her death, reflecting his love for her (Genesis 23). There is nothing in this account that validates a man abusing his wife, in any way.

Vashti and Esther

I suspect you remember the Old Testament story of Esther. (If not, do read it – it's a great tale.) But you may not remember Vashti, who makes a brief appearance in the first chapter. Both Esther and Vashti have been used – in contrasting ways – to criticise women and validate abusers.

Vashti is a disobedient wife. The queen of the king of Persia, she is summoned to attend him and his (all-male) nobles when they have all had too much to drink.

> When King Xerxes was in high spirits from wine, he commanded the seven eunuchs who served him… to bring before him Queen Vashti, wearing her royal crown, in order to display her beauty to the people and nobles, for she was lovely to look at.
> ESTHER 1:10–11

From this I would infer (as have many interpreters since ancient times) that she is to attend wearing nothing but her crown.

So, she refuses. Good on her. There is nothing in the account that suggests we should think ill of her for her refusal.

Her defiance, however, is taken seriously amiss by the king and his officials. They are very threatened by this act of female resistance.

> The queen's conduct will become known to all the women, and so they will despise their husbands.
> ESTHER 1:17

The king is so displeased that he deposes Vashti and seeks to replace her. Enter Esther, as we shall see in a moment.

Older commentators, writing within a very patriarchal worldview, agreed with the king and his counsellors that Vashti was dangerous and deserved her fate. But most modern commentators agree that Vashti should be praised for her courage. In a highly dangerous situation (the king has absolute power and she is a woman in a man's world), she refuses to be degraded as a sexual object and refuses to comply with an illegitimate demand. Not every woman is able to resist like Vashti. (Esther couldn't.) But we can applaud her for managing it.

* * *

Now we turn to Esther. I can't tell you how many times I have heard the book of Esther described as a love story or beauty pageant or heard Esther described as a model wife. None of these things is true.

Let's name it: Esther was sex-trafficked.

Probably a teenager when she entered the story, Esther was taken by force from the care of her guardian to come to the court of the king, one of a number of young women who were similarly trafficked. The king was looking to replace Vashti, and he would sleep with each of these women just once. The one who pleased him, he would make queen. The rest would be condemned to live in the king's harem for the rest of their days. They may, or may not, be recalled to the king's bed.

So Esther was brought to the palace and subjected to a lengthy series of beauty treatments, overseen by the king's eunuchs. Yes, it really is that creepy.

And this is the story of a happy marriage? This is a wife who beautifies herself for her husband. I don't think so. This is a young woman, sex-trafficked, exploited and raped. Don't let anyone tell you differently.

The wife has to consent to sex whenever the husband wants it

So far, we've looked at two of the ways in which scripture is misused by abusers who want to control or hurt their wives. Here's another to add to the list. It's the misuse of part of one of Paul's letters, mainly by men who rape or sexually coerce their wives.

Lest it needs stating, in the UK it has been illegal for a man to rape his wife for nearly 30 years, and it carries a typical sentence of 4–19 years.[19]

But does the Bible say that marital rape is acceptable? The passage that is quoted to support this view is 1 Corinthians 7:

> The wife does not have authority over her own body, but the husband does; likewise the husband does not have authority over his own body, but the wife does. Do not deprive one another except perhaps by agreement for a set time, to devote yourselves to prayer, and then come together again.
>
> 1 CORINTHIANS 7:4–5 (NRSV)

It's likely, actually, that a male abuser will only be selectively quoting part of this passage, choosing to assert his ownership over his wife's body and not the opposite. But, as in the instructions regarding mutual submission that we discussed above, here again Paul is being remarkably countercultural for his day. In a world where everyone 'knew' that a wife's body belonged to her husband, he declares that this is a mutual right. The chief force of this part of the longer passage (which, overall, is about the relative merits of singleness and marriage) is that men must learn to honour their wives' rights, not the other way around. Selective quotation actually inverts Paul's intention.

But what about Paul's comment about not depriving one another? Well, he's addressing a church which is so convinced that Jesus is about to return that they don't see much point in procreating. They are also, perhaps, influenced by various oddball strands of Christian thought (the Gnostic heresy, largely defunct now) that saw all physical activities as tainted and in conflict with the truly 'spiritual'. To this church, Paul emphasises the goodness of sexual relationships within marriage. There is not a hint here that he is speaking about rape, but simply that husband and wife should be in the habit of joyfully giving themselves to one another.

* * *

Let me make one more comment about the general argument that Paul is using throughout this letter. With reference to the many practical issues which the church is facing, he applies a common formula, 'although… do not… but rather…', which we find stated most perfectly with reference to Jesus, in Philippians 2:6–7:

> *although* he was in the form of God, he *did not* regard equality with God as something to be exploited, *but rather*, emptied himself…

This little triplet 'although [you have this entitlement], do not [stand on your rights], but rather [submit to the weaker party]' forms the paradigm for many of the pieces of advice and instruction that Paul gives.[20] In 1 Corinthians, he addresses wealthy believers (11:17–34), those who have been cheated (6:1–8), the spiritually gifted (14:26–33) and the spiritually mature (8:1–13), and he speaks of his own apostolic role (9:1–23). In each case, he urges that rights and entitlements be laid down ('although…', 'do not…') and the weaker party favoured ('but rather…').

With this in mind, it is impossible to imagine that Paul would wish to see a husband forcing his 'rights' upon a wife by raping her. What's more, in 1 Corinthians 13:5 (NRSV), Paul characterises love as 'it does not insist on its own way'. **To take his words in chapter 7 as a charter for husbands to rape or sexually coerce their wives is utterly to wrench the apostle's words from his intention.**

* * *

Lastly, we have an assortment of other scriptures used by abusers to try to keep women 'in their place'. These broadly fall under the more general category of how all women (as opposed to just wives) should be viewed, or ought to behave, and we will consider them in the next chapter.

2

The subordination of women

All women, whether married or single, are to model femininity in their various relationships, by exhibiting a distinctive modesty, responsiveness, and gentleness of spirit... We will seek to glorify God by cultivating such virtues as purity, modesty, submission, meekness, and love.

'The true woman manifesto'[21]

Jael was a woman. When the leader of the enemy army came to her tent, she must have quaked in her boots. So she slaked his thirst with fermented milk, soothed him to sleep and drove a tent peg through his skull. Meek? I don't think so. You can read that story in Judges 4 and 5.

Deborah was a woman. When God wanted his armies to fight a battle, it was Deborah that he told. She summoned the military commander and gave him his instructions. Submissive? Hardly. That story is also found in Judges 4 and 5.

Ruth was a woman. When her husband died and she found herself in a foreign land with her elderly mother-in-law to support, she knew that her husband's kinsman should marry her. So she turned up to the post-harvest carousing and seduced him (or at least, attempted to) on the threshing floor. (They don't tell you that in Sunday school!) Distinctively modest? I'm not so sure.

None of these women is criticised or censured by the biblical writers. But many people will tell you that the Bible prohibits such behaviour in women.

In this chapter we're going to look at six biblical texts that are weaponised to tell women they have to be submissive to men. We've looked at the wife–husband relationship in the previous chapter; this is about a more general impression that women should be submissive, meek and subordinate to men in general, and the abuse of scripture to tell you so.

'Women were created to help men'

> The Lord God said, 'It is not good for the man to be alone. I will make a helper suitable for him.'
> GENESIS 2:18

I used to be a doctor. In fact, I worked in hospitals for about 16 years before I was called into ministry and began theological study. Back in my day, it was a reasonably accurate generalisation that surgeons were male and theatre nurses were female – this was true in about 90% of cases. During a long operation, under the theatre lamps, the surgeon can get very warm. Occasionally they sweat so much that they need someone to mop their brow. Obviously they can't do it for themselves, because they are supposed to be sterile, so it is the duty of one of the theatre nurses to do it for the surgeon.

I think that this is the picture many people have of what is going on in Genesis here. The great man has great tasks to do, and he needs a woman standing beside him to mop his brow and cheer him on. (Please note: I'm not trying to be derogatory about theatre nurses, who perform an essential and highly skilled role, quite apart from any brow-mopping duties!)

But this just isn't accurate. The Hebrew word for 'helper' used here is *ezer*. It does not mean 'handmaiden', but rather refers to one who comes to the assistance of someone whose strength is not adequate on their own. It is most commonly used to speak of God; for example:

> God is our refuge and strength,
>   an ever-present *help* in trouble.
> PSALM 46:1

It is also used of military aid:

> When David went to Ziklag, these were the men of Manasseh who defected to him... leaders of units of a thousand in Manasseh. They *helped* David against raiding bands, for all of them were brave warriors, and they were commanders in his army.
> 1 CHRONICLES 12:20–21

So the description of the woman as a helper to the man is by no means derogatory, nor does it imply that women are incapable of acting independently of men.

'The curse of women is to be dominated by men'

> To the woman he said,
>   'I will make your pains in childbearing very severe;
>   with painful labour you will give birth to children.
>   Your desire will be for your husband,
>   and he will rule over you.'
> GENESIS 3:16

As you probably know, these are the words God addressed to Eve after she and Adam took the fruit that was forbidden to them. To Adam, God said:

> Cursed is the ground because of you;
>   through painful toil you will eat food from it
>   all the days of your life.

It will produce thorns and thistles for you,
    and you will eat the plants of the field.
By the sweat of your brow
    you will eat your food
until you return to the ground.
GENESIS 3:17–19

Historically, these words to Eve have been used to argue that a woman's suffering in childbirth is part of God's curse upon her. For example, around the turn of the 17th century a physician wrote:

In such a struggle, the mother and child feel great pains, indeed greater than all other animals. This is because of her sin, God having willed that women should give birth in pain for having been the cause of death.[22]

Such a view appears to have delayed the availability of chloroform to women in labour, even after it was being made available for surgery.

Similarly, the verse has been used to argue that women are supposed to be dominated by men: God has ordained it.

Just about nobody these days argues that women shouldn't receive pain relief in labour or, indeed, that men shouldn't use machinery to help them with cultivation. So why would we view the subordination of women as an eternal command? As Ruth Tucker says:

Some Bible interpreters argue that this curse of inequality is prescriptive for all times – that we dare not tamper with it. But the curse on the ground that meant Adam would be tilling the soil snarled with thorns and thistles has been largely reversed. Even as inventions of machinery and fertilizers have relieved the backbreaking work of agriculture, so have legal statutes mitigated the effects of gender inequality.[23]

* * *

If these words in Genesis don't mean that women should always defer to men, what's actually going on? Let's take a closer look at the passage.

First, we should notice that the language of 'curse' only applies to the snake and the soil ('Cursed are you above all livestock', v. 14; 'Cursed is the ground because of you', v. 17). Reassuringly, God does *not* curse either the man or the woman.

It is entirely reasonable, then, to read his words to the human pair as descriptive, not prescriptive; that is, 'This is what will happen as a result of your actions,' rather than, 'This is the punishment of your actions.' A bit like a parent might say to a disobedient child, 'Now look what you've done!'

It might also be helpful to notice that what we are seeing here is the disruption of God's blessing to humankind to be fruitful and multiply and exercise good governance over the earth (Genesis 1:28). Both fruitfulness and governance of the soil will now be difficult.

Again, this need not be interpreted as punishment so much as consequence.

* * *

In Genesis 1 we read that humankind was created to govern the earth with God's good rule. They were to have *dominion* over it. Now, however, the man and the woman will each seek to have dominion over one another – a mutual thirst for control.

This explains the use of the word 'desire' in verse 16. It's so often been assumed that this means sexual desire – that women are so bound to men in lust that they will be utterly in their power. We know that this is not the case because the same pair of words is used in the following chapter, where the 'desire' clearly refers to the intention to dominate.

So God says to Eve:

> Your desire [*teshukah*] shall be for your husband,
>   and he shall rule [*mashal*] over you.
>
> GENESIS 3:16 (NRSV)

And he speaks to Adam and Eve's son Cain, warning him that sin will attempt to control him:

> Sin is lurking at the door; its desire [*teshukah*] is for you, but you must master [*mashal*] it.
>
> GENESIS 4:7 (NRSV)

There is an important difference, though. In Genesis 4, God is *commanding* Cain to exercise control over sin. In Genesis 3, he is *describing* how the relationship between men and women will tend to work from now onwards.

In other words, one of the consequences of the fall is a power struggle between the sexes – one which men will often win. **But the dominance of men is not ordained by God as a punishment for women**.

'Women menstruate and are regularly unclean'

> When a woman has her regular flow of blood, the impurity of her monthly period will last seven days, and anyone who touches her will be unclean till evening.
>   Anything she lies on during her period will be unclean, and anything she sits on will be unclean. Anyone who touches her bed will be unclean; they must wash their clothes and bathe with water, and they will be unclean till evening. Anyone who touches anything she sits on will be unclean; they must wash their clothes and bathe with water, and they will be unclean till evening. Whether it is the bed or anything she was sitting on, when anyone touches it, they will be unclean till evening.
>
> LEVITICUS 15:19–23

The taboos around menstruation have contributed to a culture in some church traditions that diminishes women's self-worth. An example of this would be in the misogynistic responses experienced by some female clergy:

> You need to give me the dates of your periods so I know when not to take Communion.
>
> You won't be presiding at Communion while you're on your period, will you?[24]

We won't allow this to detain us for long, but let me just make a couple of comments.

First, Leviticus 15, where this impurity law is found, contains laws concerning both female and male uncleanness. (Uncleanness, incidentally, is not at all the same thing as guilt or sinfulness.) In addition to illnesses which caused uncleanness, there were some 'normal' events that had the same effect. In particular: a woman was made unclean by menstruation and childbirth and a man by a seminal emission, whether or not during intercourse. Here is the law concerning male uncleanness:

> When a man has an emission of semen, he must bathe his whole body with water, and he will be unclean till evening. Any clothing or leather that has semen on it must be washed with water, and it will be unclean till evening. When a man has sexual relations with a woman and there is an emission of semen, both of them must bathe with water, and they will be unclean till evening.
>
> LEVITICUS 15:16–18

By my reckoning, this would make a lot of men 'unclean' for quite a lot of the time, if this law were in force in churches today!

In actual fact, of course, the law is not in force. As the New Testament makes abundantly clear, the coming of Christ has made the law redundant. See, for example, Galatians 3:19–25, which Scot McKnight summarises as, 'Paul would say, "You cannot serve Christ and the law at the same time."'[25] So, along with Peter, we need to learn that 'what God has made clean, you must not call profane' (see Acts 10:15, NRSV).

'Women should be silent in church'

> Women should remain silent in the churches. They are not allowed to speak, but must be in submission, as the law says. If they want to enquire about something, they should ask their own husbands at home; for it is disgraceful for a woman to speak in the church.
>
> 1 CORINTHIANS 14:34–35

A long while ago, I was in conversation with someone who was describing a church they attended which took these verses at their literal face value. She – and yes, it was a woman – was telling me that women weren't allowed to pray in their church meetings. 'I mean, they are allowed to pray,' she clarified hastily, 'just not aloud.' I was so horrified at this comment that I still remember it about 30 years later. Because, of course, *everyone* is permitted to pray! This should never be in doubt – it goes without saying. Only in that church, apparently, it didn't.

As you will know, or might guess, these few verses from the first letter to the church in Corinth are the source of a huge amount of discussion and debate. Different Christians can have different views on these verses, with utter integrity. Obviously a full discussion of this text would require a whole book, or more, but let me offer five views to show the range of interpretive options.

Option 1: Paul meant that women should never speak in church. This is difficult to sustain in the light of Paul's words just a few chapters earlier:

> Every woman who prays or prophesies with her head uncovered dishonours her head.
> 1 CORINTHIANS 11:5

I therefore find this option utterly implausible.

Option 2: Paul permits women to prophesy and pray in church but forbids them to teach. This position is proposed by the well-respected conservative scholar Don Carson. His interpretation allows women many speaking roles in church but does not allow them to have a recognised teaching role when men are present. However, he emphasises the countercultural nature of Paul's words:

> In a Greek *ekklesia* [public meeting], women were not allowed to speak at all. By contrast, women in the Christian *ekklesia* [church], borne along by the Spirit, were *encouraged* to do so.[26]

Carson's position is carefully argued and thoughtful, though I do question whether it is really possible to argue that women did not teach men in the early church, particularly in the light of the prominence given to Priscilla (female) in the teaching of Apollos (male):

> [Apollos] knew only the baptism of John. He began to speak boldly in the synagogue. When Priscilla and Aquila heard him, they invited him to their home and explained to him the way of God more adequately.
> ACTS 18:25–26

Option 3: Paul is here calling for order in the conduct of worship. By this argument, Paul makes his remarks because women were being disorderly in worship, calling out and chatting among themselves. We believe that women sat separately from men in the early churches and would have received a lower level of education than some men. These two factors may have led to them feeling more like spectators than participants. Spectators are more likely to chat among themselves.

In favour of this argument is the wider context of Paul's remarks. A key theme in 1 Corinthians 12—14 is order in worship. One of the issues causing problems in that church was the abandoning of all restraint in response to the gospel of freedom that they had received. (This may also relate to Paul's instructions to women to cover their heads in worship. Failure to do so was making them look like 'loose women', which was bringing the church into disrepute.)

By this argument, then, women were to be settled and restrained during worship but were not prevented from contributing constructively. Broadly speaking, this is the interpretation favoured by Tom Wright.[27]

Option 4: Paul is quoting something that the Corinthians had written to him. We already know that Paul does this a few times in the Corinthian letters. He quotes from their letter to him and then disagrees with them. We see this in 1 Corinthians 6:12; 7:1; 8:1, 8; 10:23.

As this argument goes, Paul is quoting their letter, which said women should keep silent, and then responds with a sarcastic rebuttal. I paraphrase, 'Did the word of God originate with you men only? Or are you the only ones it has reached?' This case is well made by Kirk MacGregor.[28]

Option 5: Paul never wrote these words at all. We don't have Paul's original letter, sadly, but only a collection of copies. And probably none of these were direct copies from the original. Sometimes minor errors crept in with the copying process, and occasionally a presumptuous scribe inserted or omitted something to 'correct' what he understood to be an error.

Several very eminent scholars, including the well-respected Gordon Fee,[29] take the view that these verses are not original to Paul but have been added later by a scribe who wanted to align the letter with his own particular ideology of women. There is good, but not watertight, evidence for this position.

* * *

I'm sorry that I can't give you a definite answer on this one. Personally, I tend towards options 3 or 4. For me, the evidence that women were very active in all aspects of ministry in the early church is just too persuasive to allow me to be convinced by options 1 and 2, not to mention that women were the first witnesses to the resurrection – in a world where a woman's testimony was automatically suspect.

However, what I most want to persuade you of is this: there is enough ambiguity about the interpretation of these verses that it is frankly dangerous to pin a whole theology of gender roles on to them. And – more importantly – there is nothing here, even in the most conservative interpretations, that implies that women should be subservient to or are of lesser value than men.

'Women were deceived and are inherently unreliable'

> Let a woman learn in silence with full submission. I permit no woman to teach or to have authority over a man; she is to keep silent. For Adam was formed first, then Eve; and Adam was not deceived, but the woman was deceived and became a transgressor. Yet she will be saved through childbearing, provided they continue in faith and love and holiness, with modesty.
>
> 1 TIMOTHY 2:11–15 (NRSV)

This has long been viewed as the most problematic passage of all in terms of our understanding of Paul's attitude to, and teaching about, women. The reason is that he appears to give a theological explanation for his words, which makes it harder to argue that he is only addressing a particular church context.

However, there are some really important things to say about this passage. The first one is that the only direct instruction is in the first few words: 'Let a woman learn.' This was hugely countercultural – just think about the fuss made when Mary came and sat at Jesus' feet like one of the 'real' disciples (Luke 10:38–42).

Next we need to set out a bit of the background to the letter. It is being written to Timothy, pastor of the church in Ephesus. There were some particular things about the church in Ephesus that might help us understand Paul's words better:

- The main religion in Ephesus was a female-only cult which worshipped the goddess Artemis. The priests of Artemis were all women.
- The letter is probably being written around the time that the Gnostic heresy was emerging. The Gnostics believed that the spiritual things were of much greater value than physical things. Ideally, one would cast off one's physical being altogether. In particular, there were Gnostic elements that believed that childbearing would cause a woman to lose her salvation.
- Another of the false truths being put about in those days was that Eve had been created before Adam, but Adam was deceived into believing that it was the other way around. Obviously this is in direct contradiction to the order of creation as described in Genesis 2.

Now, if we bear those three things in mind, Paul's instructions could be paraphrased like this:

> Let women learn, in submission to God. I will not allow the women in the church in Ephesus to teach or rule the men, as they do in the Artemis temple. Because they are wrong in saying Eve was created first; it was Adam. And it is they who have been deceived about this matter, not Adam. Moreover, if they become pregnant, their salvation will not be lost in childbearing, if they continue living in a godly manner.

This interpretation has been proposed by Catherine and Richard Kroeger[30] and has been adopted by many, but not all, scholars who consider these matters. Once again, however, the ambiguity around the meaning makes it inappropriate to be dogmatic about its interpretation, particularly if that interpretation lends itself to the subordination of half of the human race.

* * *

We looked briefly in the previous chapter at the different opinions regarding the submission of wives to their husbands. In this chapter we have been thinking about the submission of women in general. Nowhere in scripture does it say that women should submit to men in general. And nowhere does it say that women are inferior in worth.

Yet, tragically, this is not how churches always teach about such matters. Catherine and Richard Kroeger tell some sad stories at the beginning of their book:

> A physician in family practice was summoned to her pastor's study and there was informed that her chosen medical specialty is outside God's will for her life. The pastor insisted that only two specialties are open to her: obstetrics/gynecology and pediatrics. The electrified young woman asked why God could not see fit to use her gifts in implementing healing for families. The answer was that 1 Timothy 2:12 forbade her have any authority over men, and therefore she could not enter into a patient/physician relationship with a man. The woman left the church.

An attorney was told by certain members of her family that according to 1 Timothy 2:11–15 she should be a waitress rather than a lawyer.

A church magazine announced that a dedicated laywoman would take over the leadership of a ministry to nursing homes in the Milwaukee area. An indignant reader responded, 'Exactly how does the "headship" given her square with 1 Timothy 2:11–15?'[31]

But these represent plain bad theology, whichever way you interpret the texts we have been looking at. Even 'complementarian' theologians who affirm the submission of wives acknowledge that this does not extend to all women: 'Paul does not ask every woman to submit to every man.'[32]

More than this, complementarian theology, as egalitarian theology, affirms that women are no less valuable in the sight of God. This is a quotation from the 'Nashville statement', produced by the Council on Biblical Manhood and Womanhood:

We affirm that God created Adam and Eve, the first human beings, in his own image, *equal before God as persons*, and distinct as male and female. We deny that the divinely ordained differences between male and female render them unequal in dignity or worth.[33]

* * *

It has not been my purpose in this chapter to comment in detail on the 'women in church ministry' question. My own biography on the back of this book will give you a clue to the stance that I take on the matter. But that is not what matters here. What I hope I have persuaded you of is that the Bible is not stacked against you. It is not colluding with your abusive husband that you are inferior and of little worth. As we shall see in chapter 8, the truth is quite the opposite.

3

Divorce

God hates divorce, and therefore hates me if I get divorced.

Abuse survivor, interview transcript

Malachi

In this chapter we are going to look at one of the scriptures that is sometimes used to convince women to return to their husbands. This is Malachi 2:16, 'I hate divorce, says the Lord' (NRSV).

By means of the use (misuse, as we shall see) of this verse, the woman – who has perhaps just built up enough courage to disclose the abuse and seek help for the first time – is told she must stay in the marriage and in the marital home. Or if she separates it should only be for a short time, pending a reconciliation. Because God hates divorce. End of conversation.

But it really isn't the end of the conversation, for all sorts of reasons, as I will try to show you.

* * *

First, this is a notoriously difficult passage to translate. Compare the NRSV with the NIV translation:

> For I hate divorce, says the Lord, the God of Israel, and covering one's garment with violence, says the Lord of hosts. (NRSV)

'The man who hates and divorces his wife,' says the Lord, the God of Israel, 'does violence to the one he should protect,' says the Lord Almighty. (NIV)

You might be excused for thinking that you were reading different verses (I had to double-check when I was copying these verses in). As you can see, that oft-quoted snippet, 'I hate divorce,' does not even occur in some translations.

* * *

But let's look at this verse in its context and in more detail. If we are to understand how this passage might be relevant for us, we first need to understand exactly what the prophet is and isn't saying to his original audience.

Malachi the prophet is writing in the time of post-exilic Israel. In other words, he is addressing the ancient nation of Israel after their conquest and deportation by the Babylonians, at the time when the scattered people are making their way back to Jerusalem. They are trying to re-establish a godly way of living. This is Malachi's situation and Malachi's audience. He was not talking to 21st-century people.

Now, notice this: Malachi is predominantly talking to men. We know this because in verses 14 and 15, he three times refers to 'your wives'. And although divorce was in principle available to women,[34] in practice this would almost certainly have been hard for a woman to achieve.

So to the man – the one with the power – God says:

The Lord is the witness between you and the wife of your youth.
v. 14

That covenant of marriage is very important indeed.

So if God says, 'I hate divorce', doesn't that make it an absolute prohibition to all people at all times?

The social context can help us here. In the ancient world, a woman who was unmarried and not a virgin was regarded as unmarriageable. If she were a widow, she might be able to remarry. But a woman divorced by her husband, for no fault of her own, would likely be viewed by other men – appallingly – as 'spoiled goods'. She would probably not be able to remarry. And so she would be without a protector and at risk of destitution or of having to take the most desperate measures to avoid it. Unless she had a well-disposed male relative, she would be vulnerable to anyone who chose to take advantage of her and would have to do whatever it took to make ends meet. Let's name it – she would probably have to resort to sex work in order to provide for herself and her children.

So yes, God does appear to hate divorce, because he cares about the protection of vulnerable women and their children.

* * *

We'll take a quick detour to the Hebrew used here, but we won't linger long. There are three important words and ideas in this short passage, all linked: *bagad* – to deal treacherously; *berit* – covenant; and *hamas* – violence.

Bagad is translated 'to be faithless' in most versions. Three times (verses 14, 15 and 16) Malachi accuses the men of faithlessness or, more literally, dealing treacherously with their wives. *Bagad* refers to someone who breaks a covenant (e.g. Judges 9:23). It is most commonly used of situations in society where one person breaks faith with another. It is also used of Israel's disobedience to God. A few times it is used in the context of marriage, for acting treacherously in marriage. And in particular (v. 14), it refers to breaking the covenant (*berit*) of marriage – the solemn, binding contract. As David Instone-Brewer says:

Verse 16 shows that God is against the person who breaks one's marriage vows... The constantly reiterated theme of these verses is faithfulness to the terms of the marriage covenant. *Criticism is not directed at the person who carries out the divorce but at the person who causes the divorce* by not being faithful to the marriage covenant.[35]

What constitutes a breach of the marriage covenant? Adultery is clearly one of them. But, unexpectedly, Malachi emphasises another one. Because he suddenly uses the word *hamas*, violence.

As I said, the correct translation of verse 16 is tricky, because the Hebrew is grammatically odd. I think the verse is best translated:

For I hate divorce, says the Lord, the God of Israel, and him who covers his garment with violence, says the Lord of hosts.

What does it mean, to cover one's garments withviolence? It may be referring to the marriage custom of the day, where a man appears to have taken the woman under his cloak as a sign of her entering his protection (see Ruth 3:9). Malachi is referring to the bringing of violence into the marital home. *This* constitutes a breach of the marriage covenant.

Divorce and abuse: God hates them both. If God hates the 'sending away' of a wife, God hates violence against her, too. God hates it when men are violent to their wives, when they coercively control them, and he equally hates it when they abuse their power and privilege to cast them out without protection.

* * *

This is a difficult passage and there are lots of areas of uncertainty. Let me summarise the take-home message:

- The best translation of these verses is unclear, and as a result some of the fine details are quite ambiguous. Therefore it is inappropriate to use it dogmatically.
- Husbands were being condemned for acting treacherously towards their wives, using the language of a covenant breach and with reference to violence.
- The divorce that God is described as hating appears to refer primarily to endangering a (vulnerable) woman by 'sending her away'.

In other words, this passage in Malachi is all about protecting wives: protecting them from destitution and protecting them from violence. **To use it to manipulate a woman into staying with an abusive husband is an *exact inversion* of its original purpose.**

Jesus and the rabbis

But what about Jesus? Didn't he advance this divorce theme further?

Yes, of course he did. The sermon on the mount is all about the extension of Old Testament law into new covenant ethics. Jesus speaks about divorce both there and more fully in a conversation with the Pharisees. The conversation with the Pharisees, as reported by Matthew, is the fullest discussion of the situation:

> Some Pharisees came to him, and to test him they asked, 'Is it lawful for a man to divorce his wife *for any cause*?'
>
> MATTHEW 19:3 (NRSV, my italics)

The question that the Pharisees put to Jesus relates to a theological debate of the day. There was more than one rabbinic school of thought about divorce. One side argued that a man could not divorce his wife except for adultery. By contrast, the other side said that a husband could divorce his wife for 'any matter' – a technical legal term which meant that a husband did not have to provide any grounds for divorce and could get rid of his wife on a whim.[36]

So the Pharisees were asking Jesus his opinion about a hot topic: 'Do you agree with the "any matter" clause?' And as was so often the case, Jesus' reply did not immediately answer the question. Instead he quoted Genesis 1, to point to God's intention for marriage to be monogamous and lifelong:

> He answered, 'Have you not read that the one who made them at the beginning "made them male and female", and said, "For this reason a man shall leave his father and mother and be joined to his wife, and the two shall become one flesh"? So they are no longer two, but one flesh. Therefore what God has joined together, let no one separate.'
>
> MATTHEW 19:4–6 (NRSV)

But the Pharisees wanted an answer to their question, so they pressed him further:

> 'Why then,' they asked, 'did Moses command that a man give his wife a certificate of divorce and send her away?'
>
> MATTHEW 19:7

The law they were referring to is in Deuteronomy:

> If a man marries a woman who becomes displeasing to him because he finds something indecent about her, and he writes her a certificate of divorce, gives it to her and sends her from his house, and if after she leaves his house she becomes the wife of another man, and her second husband dislikes her and writes her a certificate of divorce, gives it to her and sends her from his house, or if he dies, *then her first husband, who divorced her, is not allowed to marry her again* after she has been defiled. That would be detestable in the eyes of the Lord.
>
> DEUTERONOMY 24:1–4 (my italics)

Notice that this law is not about the legality of divorce but is address-ing the question of *remarriage after divorce*. And Jesus' reply needs to be understood in this context. First, he reasserted that divorce is not God's best purpose:

> Jesus replied, 'Moses permitted you to divorce your wives because your hearts were hard. But it was not this way from the beginning.'
> MATTHEW 19:8

Then he addressed the question of remarriage after divorce:

> I tell you that anyone who divorces his wife, except for sexual immorality, and marries another woman commits adultery.
> MATTHEW 19:9

In other words, Jesus is addressing the question of remarriage after divorce. **He is not saying that the only grounds for divorce is adultery.**

* * *

If you are still in doubt, take a look at how Paul interprets Jesus' words in the same way:

> To the married I give this command (not I, but the Lord): a wife must not separate from her husband. But if she does, she must remain unmarried or else be reconciled to her husband. And a husband must not divorce his wife.
> 1 CORINTHIANS 7:10–11

In other words, Paul says that separation from a husband is not ideal but permissible.

* * *

We should be expecting Jesus to take this stance, because we know he didn't contradict the Old Testament law (though he did extend it).[37] And Old Testament law permitted a woman to divorce her husband on the grounds of deprivation of food or clothing, or on the grounds of abandonment (Exodus 21:10–11).

This conversation has led many highly respected theologians (including the great Augustine) to argue that there are a number of forms of mistreatment which constitute equally strong grounds for divorce as adultery.

Even the conservative, complementarian scholar Wayne Grudem has come around to this way of thinking. Having argued for years that the only biblically sanctioned grounds for divorce are adultery and desertion, at the November 2019 meeting of the Evangelical Theological Society he demonstrated a surprising change of mind. His argument is centred on 1 Corinthians 7:15, 'If the unbelieving partner separates, let him separate. In such cases the brother or sister is not enslaved. God has called you to peace.'[38] Careful study of the Greek phrase here translated 'in such cases' has led Grudem to conclude that abandonment by an unbelieving spouse is not the only circumstance which Paul has in mind. He says:

> 'In such cases' should be understood to include *any* cases that similarly destroy a marriage.[39]

Grudem therefore concludes that behaviours which constitute equally strong grounds for divorce include: extreme prolonged verbal and relational cruelty, credible threats of physical harm, incorrigible drug, alcohol or gambling addiction, and habitual pornography use.

Or, as another theologian has written:

> Although it is evident that adultery affects the marriage relation more closely than any other offence, yet it may fairly be said that there are other things which may make married life

so intolerable, and the perfect ideal union so impossible, that, if divorce or separation be allowed at all, the grounds for such separation ought not in reason to be confined to the one offence of adultery.[40]

This makes sense, and it is in line with what we've already seen in Malachi. Adultery goes to the heart of what a marriage really is, and it is easy to see how it breaks the marriage covenant. But neglect, abandonment and abuse also strike against the covenant of marriage. And it seems to me that nothing Jesus says would contradict this.

Isn't that just what we would expect of Jesus? An uncompromising call to holy living and a shepherd's heart for the hurt and violated.

And does God hate divorce? I believe he hates every breach of the marriage covenant – whether through violence, abuse, abandonment, neglect or adultery – and he weeps that divorce is sometimes a necessary expression of that.

4

Forgiveness and suffering

Early in our marriage I went to a clergyman who, after a few visits, told me that my husband meant no real harm, he was just confused and insecure. So I was encouraged to be more tolerant and understanding. Most important, I was told to forgive him the beatings just as Christ had forgiven from the cross.

Abuse survivor[41]

What is forgiveness and what isn't it?

One of the things that sets the Christian faith apart is the radical call to forgiveness and to enemy-love that Jesus makes:

> You have heard that it was said, 'Love your neighbour and hate your enemy.' But I tell you, love your enemies and pray for those who persecute you, that you may be children of your Father in heaven. He causes his sun to rise on the evil and the good, and sends rain on the righteous and the unrighteous.
> MATTHEW 5:43–45

> Forgive us our debts, as we also have forgiven our debtors… For if you forgive other people when they sin against you, your heavenly Father will also forgive you. But if you do not forgive others their sins, your Father will not forgive your sins.
> MATTHEW 6:12–15

> Peter came to Jesus and asked, 'Lord, how many times shall I forgive my brother or sister who sins against me? Up to seven times?' Jesus answered, 'I tell you, not seven times, but seventy-seven times.'
> MATTHEW 18:21–22

There's no way around this. If we are to be followers of Jesus, we have to learn to forgive, as we ourselves have been forgiven.

But what does forgiveness actually mean? What does it include and what does it not? Here are some of the untruths that I regularly hear (spoken or implied) about forgiveness:

- Forgiveness is easy – just get on and do it
- Forgiveness means you have to restore the relationship with the person who hurt you
- Forgiveness means you need to make yourself available to be hurt again.
- Being forgiven means that the consequences of your actions are now nullified.

These are not true. Forgiveness is not easy. Forgiveness does not mean the relationship must be restored to what it was. Forgiveness does not mean you have to make yourself available to be hurt again.

One of the best writers on this subject is Miroslav Volf.[42] He writes as an academic, but one who has experienced major pain within his family, and who saw his parents forgive those whose gross negligence caused the death of his five-year-old brother.

Volf urges that human forgiveness must be modelled on God's own forgiveness:

> The world is sinful. That's why God doesn't affirm it indiscriminately. God loves the world. That's why God doesn't punish it in justice. What does God do with the double-bind? God forgives.[43]

In other words, God doesn't look at human sin and say, 'Never mind, it doesn't matter.' Because it does matter. The cross is the measure of how much it matters.

And so our forgiveness, too, is not a denial that we were wronged. It is not a fingers-crossed-behind-the-back assertion that everything is now 'back to normal'. When we forgive:

> … we do two main things: We claim that the offender has offended us, and we don't count the offense against the offender. Both are essential. Drop not counting the offense against the offender, and all you're left with is the accusation. Drop the claim that an offense was committed, and all you have is disregard of the offense, not its forgiveness.[44]

Forgiveness is a choice not to seek vengeance. It is not a denial that the offence took place. To seek vengeance is to be overcome by the evil that the other person is seeking to draw you into.

> Do not repay anyone evil for evil. Be careful to do what is right in the eyes of everyone. If it is possible, as far as it depends on you, live at peace with everyone. Do not take revenge, my dear friends, but leave room for God's wrath, for it is written: 'It is mine to avenge; I will repay,' says the Lord. On the contrary: 'If your enemy is hungry, feed him; if he is thirsty, give him something to drink. In doing this, you will heap burning coals on his head.' Do not be overcome by evil, but overcome evil with good.
> ROMANS 12:17–21

* * *

But forgiveness does not prevent due process. Here is Jesus speaking in answer to the hypothetical situation, 'What do I do if my brother sins against me?':

'If your brother or sister sins, go and point out their fault, just between the two of you. If they listen to you, you have won them over. But if they will not listen, take one or two others along, so that "every matter may be established by the testimony of two or three witnesses." If they still refuse to listen, tell it to the church; and if they refuse to listen even to the church, treat them as you would a pagan or a tax collector…'

Then Peter came to Jesus and asked, 'Lord, how many times shall I forgive my brother or sister who sins against me? Up to seven times?' Jesus answered, 'I tell you, not seven times, but seventy-seven times.'

MATTHEW 18:15-17, 21-22

What do I do if someone sins against me? Twice in short succession Jesus answers the same question. Once he points to church discipline (and, ultimately, to exclusion). The second time he speaks about forgiveness. Did he have a memory lapse or change his mind? Of course not! We can conclude, therefore, that there is no conflict between following due process and forgiving within your heart.

Jesus' words about putting someone out of the church also show that there is no objection to keeping a safe distance away from the abuser – if necessary, indefinitely. It does not, however, get you out of the challenge to come to a place of forgiveness.

Forgiveness cannot and should not be rushed into. Part of the healing process after someone has abused you is coming to terms with your own pain. There is often a stage of denial about the full impact that the abuse has had. It is important to make space to acknowledge the pain that you have suffered before you can journey towards forgiveness.

Nor is forgiveness an instantaneous event. Human experience tells us this. We can find ourselves needing to forgive the same person for the same crime on a daily basis – maybe on an hourly basis. It *does* become easier, eventually and with practice. But forgiveness is a process, not an event.

I wonder if we get a tiny clue about this in the crucifixion account. You'll be familiar, I'm sure, with Jesus' prayer about his torturers, 'Father, forgive them' (Luke 23:34). But the Greek tense that is used (the imperfect) implies that Jesus *kept saying*, 'Father, forgive them.' Is it possible that even Jesus needed to keep re-forgiving as the agony continued? I dare not assert it as fact, but I wonder.

* * *

One of the texts that is used in relation to forgiveness is 'turn the other cheek'. Isn't this a clear instruction to allow the abuser to carry on?

The first thing to say is that I am sure we are to imagine this situation playing out between two men, not between a man and a woman. We'll return to the woman–man thing in a minute. First let's think about it with regard to two men.

Walter Wink offers a helpful interpretation of these words. He notes that in Matthew's gospel, Jesus stipulates that it is the *right* cheek which has been assaulted. Now, work out how two people would have to be standing for this to work. How does a right-handed person strike you on the right cheek? By backhanding you. This is not a punch between equals but the backhanded blow that one might give an inferior – a slave, perhaps.

And in response to this action – both assault and insult – Jesus instructs that his listeners should offer their other cheek, their left cheek. *That* is an invitation to be struck as an equal.

Wink's interpretation of Jesus' words is this: if one man assaults another man as an inferior, in a humiliating and derogatory way, the man who has been backhanded might invite the other one to strike him again, as an equal. It is a call to radical non-violence, but by taking control of the situation, rather than being controlled by it.

The person who turns the other cheek is saying, in effect, 'Try again. Your first blow failed to achieve its intended effect. I deny you the power to humiliate me. I am a human being just like you. Your status does not alter that fact. You cannot demean me.'[45]

What might this look like when a man hits his wife? The first thing to say is that you only have two cheeks! Many men have assaulted their wives many more times than twice. So if we were to take this literally, most women who experience abuse have already more than satisfied this instruction.

But if we follow Walter Wink's line of reasoning, then the words of Jesus are an invitation to women who are assaulted in this way to look their abusers in the eye and assert their own worth and value.

Jesus is not referring to repeated submission to abuse, but to making a voluntary, empowered decision about what to permit – *or not*. The choice is yours and no one else's.

Let me emphasise something at this point. I am not trying to provide a blueprint for how a woman should respond to a violent husband. Only you can judge the likely risks, and you should prioritise your own safety and that of any children who are involved. I am just trying to debunk certain misunderstandings about what Jesus asks us to do. In particular, I am trying to help you to see that he is not telling you that you just have to put up with abuse. Turning the other cheek doesn't mean allowing your abuser to beat you half to death.

To reiterate, to forgive your abuser does not mean that you have to allow him to hurt you all over again. And your decision whether to stay or leave should be free and uncoerced.

This brings us to the next question, the next misunderstanding that sometimes traps women in relationships with abusive men: the question of suffering and Christian discipleship.

Suffering and the Christian vocation

> I was told that suffering was part of my 'holy burden' as a woman.
>
> Abuse survivor, interview transcript

I'm sorry if – like the lady I interviewed whom I quote above – you have been told this as a way of making you tolerate the intolerable.

It's true that the New Testament does speak a lot about Christians suffering. And sometimes, it seems as if the apostles assumed that suffering is normal, something to be expected. But when they imply this, they are not talking about random suffering or abuse. They are speaking about the persecution that many followers of Jesus face in every age.

In the situation of Christian persecution, the way of faithfulness will often require patient endurance, because in general the only way out of that sort of suffering is to deny Jesus. But even persecution is not something to be embraced without hoping and praying and striving for a way out. So although James emphasises the character development that persecution can bring about…

> Consider it pure joy, my brothers and sisters, whenever you face trials of many kinds, because you know that the testing of your faith produces perseverance. Let perseverance finish its work so that you may be mature and complete, not lacking anything.
>
> JAMES 1:2–4

… on the other hand, Peter and Paul both accept their release from prison when it is offered to them (e.g. Acts 12:9; 16:35–40). Paul uses his Roman citizenship to avoid a flogging – and seriously embarrass the officials at the same time (Acts 22:25).

But not all suffering is persecution. For example, in relation to something that might be closer to domestic abuse, Paul urges slaves to gain their freedom if they can (1 Corinthians 7:21). There is no hint that they should remain in their position in order to suffer as an expression of their Christian duty. The Bible does not call us to be masochists.

* * *

Notice this, too. Who is it who makes those bold calls to suffer under persecution? (Not random abuse, mind, but persecution for the faith.)

> Whoever wants to be my disciple must deny themselves and take up their cross and follow me.
> MATTHEW 16:24

> Consider it pure joy, my brothers and sisters, whenever you face trials of many kinds.
> JAMES 1:2

> Who is going to harm you if you are eager to do good? But even if you should suffer for what is right, you are blessed. 'Do not fear their threats; do not be frightened.' But in your hearts revere Christ as Lord.
> 1 PETER 3:13–15

> You then, my son, be strong in the grace that is in Christ Jesus… Join with me in suffering.
> 2 TIMOTHY 2:1, 3

In the order that I have listed them, they are: Jesus (crucified); James (martyred – probably thrown from the top of the temple and stoned); Peter (crucified); Paul (beheaded).[46] I can think of no instance where someone calls for the patient endurance of persecution who does not stand in dire peril of that same fate themselves. *And* the words are being spoken by apostles, or by the Lord himself.

This bears no resemblance to an abuser, or a bystander, telling someone to endure domestic abuse. Nobody has the right to do that.

A lament

As an antidote to thoughtless or manipulative instructions to forgive easily and to bear up under suffering, I'd like to offer you the beautiful and tender Psalm 55. It's not one of the better-known ones, so it may be unfamiliar to you. I hope you will find it helpful, and you may like to use it as a prayer.

I'll give some highlights here, but do take a look at the full version from your preferred translation. Some of the parts I've removed are rather strongly worded prayers against the enemy. You will need to take a view on how you wish to use them.[47] It's certainly fine to pray for the frustration of an abuser's plans to harm you.

I suspect that the original writer was male, but as the psalm belongs to all the people of God, let's put it into a female voice. The psalmist begins by appealing to God for help. She has been sorely pressed by someone who feels like an enemy:

> Listen to my prayer, O God,
>> do not ignore my plea;
>> hear me and answer me.
> My thoughts trouble me and I am distraught
>> because of what my enemy is saying,
>> because of the threats of the wicked;
> for they bring down suffering on me
>> and assail me in their anger.

Her language intensifies. She is not afraid to express the depth of her anguish to God, because she knows that he is listening and that he cares:

> My heart is in anguish within me;
>> the terrors of death have fallen on me.
> Fear and trembling have beset me;
>> horror has overwhelmed me.

She fantasises about being able to escape:

> I said, 'Oh, that I had the wings of a dove!
>   I would fly away and be at rest.
> I would flee far away
>   and stay in the desert;
> I would hurry to my place of shelter,
>   far from the tempest and storm.'

She prays that the one who threatens her will be frustrated in his designs:

> Lord, confuse the wicked, confound their words,
>   for I see violence and strife in the city.

But suddenly it becomes clear to us. Her 'enemy' is not a stranger, but one who is near, one who is or was dear. She expresses grief at this betrayal:

> If an enemy were insulting me,
>   I could endure it;
> if a foe were rising against me,
>   I could hide.
> But it is you, my equal,[48]
>   my companion, my close friend,
> with whom I once enjoyed sweet fellowship
>   at the house of God,
> as we walked about
>   among the worshippers.

She expresses again her confidence that God has not forgotten her:

> As for me, I call to God,
>   and the Lord saves me.
> Evening, morning and noon
>   I cry out in distress,
>   and he hears my voice.

She returns again to the theme of her betrayal by a loved one – one who has broken the solemn promises that he once made. Her words speak very eloquently about the coercive control she has experienced:

My companion attacks his friends;
   he violates his covenant.
His talk is smooth as butter,
   yet war is in his heart.

She reminds herself, even though circumstances now are bleak, to put her trust in God. He has not forgotten her:

Cast your cares on the Lord
   and he will sustain you;
he will never let
   the righteous be shaken.

May the Lord indeed sustain you. And may he give you, if you desire them, wings like a dove to fly away to a place of shelter.

5

When pastor turns predator

The man who abused me used to say it was God's will, and that I had to obey him, because he was God's holy representative.
Abuse survivor[49]

Once upon a time there was a man, a charismatic leader of God's people. He was hugely gifted and capable of inspiring people to follow him. Through him, God did amazing things. But at home, things were not so good. He had one daughter, an only child, whom he loved dearly. Or, at least, he said that he loved her. But she always came second to his work. When it came to the question of what was most important to him, he chose his position, his power and his success. And he was willing to sacrifice his daughter to achieve his ambitions. Quite literally. He killed her as an offering to the deity that he had come to imagine that God was.

His name was Jephthah, but his daughter's name is not recorded. You can find her story in Judges 11. Jephthah is a classic case of a gifted charismatic leader who abused his family. Character does not always match up to giftedness.

* * *

Churches and denominations vary in how they view their leaders. In my own (UK) Baptist church family, ministers are answerable to the church meeting, a system which provides 'checks and balances' for the use of power. In some other denominations, the leader has a lot more power and control over the congregation.[50]

It is widely recognised that there is a triple temptation that lurks at the edge of all Christian leadership. If one of these three isn't a temptation to the leader, another probably will be. This triple temptation is: money, sex and power. Being a minister (or priest, or vicar, or pastor, or elder, or whatever name your particular denomination uses) presents peculiar pressures, and tragically not all ministers manage to withstand them.

Fortunately, the majority of Christian ministers are men and women of God – flawed but sincere, humble and prayerful. But when ministers take a wrong turn, when they start to exercise spiritual abuse, it can be very damaging indeed.

It can be damaging for a number of reasons. One reason is the spiritual authority that is placed in their hands. A church leader who abuses his spouse is likely to also harm his church, as God is unlikely to bless the ministry of a church leader who is living in flagrant disobedience. (It may appear to succeed for a while, but it will not stand in the end – see 1 Corinthians 3:10–17.) Another reason is the power that accompanies church leadership. Ministers get to hear secrets, they have the power to make people feel encouraged or crushed and they interpret scripture to the people.

* * *

In the 16th century, the brilliant and courageous William Tyndale began to translate the Bible into English. He was passionate that everyone in the land – down to the boy who ploughed the field – should be able to read the Bible for themselves. The church establishment fiercely opposed him in this, as did Henry VIII's government. Tyndale fled to the continent and worked there, on the run. Eventually he was betrayed by a friend and ended up paying for his obedience to God with his life – but not before all of the New Testament and half of the Old Testament had been smuggled into the country and had made their way, via the printing presses, into the hands of ordinary people.

Why were the authorities so keen to ban the translation of the Bible into a language that people could read? Because it would take power out of the hands of the priests. They knew that the person who controls the interpretation of the Bible can control the people who believe it.

This means that an abusive minister (or vicar, or priest, etc.) carries with them a particularly potent way of making people fall into line. We have, tragically, seen this in the many and continually emerging stories of clergy sexually abusing children and women.

I began this book by quoting 'Jenny', whose husband abused her verbally, physically and sexually for decades. He was the one who interpreted scripture to her, and he used it as a means of controlling her.

In Jenny's case, her husband's physical abuse of her was exacerbated and facilitated because he also exercised spiritual abuse against her.

* * *

One of the recurring themes that I have heard as I have been listening to survivors of domestic abuse within churches, and as I have been reading blogs and following social media, is this one. With reference to making an accusation against a church minister, the accusers are told: 'Touch not the Lord's anointed.'

In other words, 'If you make this accusation, you are hindering the work of God. If the pastor is doing God's work, anyone who contradicts him must be opposed to God. Anyone who contradicts him or accuses him of abuse is working for Satan. Therefore, "touch not the Lord's anointed".'

But is this scriptural? Let's take a good look at this and see if it stands up to scrutiny.

First let's look at the place where that little phrase is found. It's in Psalm 105:15. We'll take a few verses to put it in context:

He is the Lord our God;
    his judgements are in all the earth.
He remembers his covenant forever,
    the promise he made, for a thousand generations,
the covenant he made with Abraham,
    the oath he swore to Isaac.
He confirmed it to Jacob as a decree,
    to Israel as an everlasting covenant:
'To you I will give the land of Canaan
    as the portion you will inherit.'
When they were but few in number,
    few indeed, and strangers in it,
they wandered from nation to nation,
    from one kingdom to another.
He allowed no one to oppress them;
    for their sake he rebuked kings:
'*Do not touch my anointed ones*;
    do my prophets no harm.'

PSALM 105:7–15 (my italics)

What do we notice? First, this is a psalm. It is a worship song – in this instance a song of praise and of history telling. The psalmist is recalling the days of the patriarchs, Abraham, Isaac and Jacob. There is no instruction given – neither to the ancient reader nor to us. This is not law and it is not prophecy.

Second, who were these 'anointed ones' who were not to be touched? They weren't church leaders! They weren't even national leaders. The psalmist is talking about the family of Abraham, long in the past, even for him. He is poetically saying that they should be protected from local warlords (like Abimelek and Ephron: see Genesis 21:22–34 and 23:10–20). The verse is talking about God protecting *all* his people.

It takes a peculiar sort of mental gymnastics – or a cynically manipulative use of scripture – to convert this into a command against calling a church leader to account.

There are a couple of stories in the book of Samuel that might be seen to lend a little more support, though the quotation used above is not found in either of them.

In 1 Samuel 24, we are told of David hiding from King Saul in a cave, when Saul came into the cave to relieve himself. David had Saul at his mercy and could very easily have killed him. (David had been on the run from Saul's murderous intentions for a long while.) Instead, David cut off a portion of Saul's cloak and then felt guilty for his action:

> 'The Lord forbid that I should do this thing to my lord, the Lord's anointed, to raise my hand against him; for he is the Lord's anointed.'
> 1 SAMUEL 24:6 (NRSV)

'To raise my hand against him' – this is a reference to violent action. A very similar story takes place two chapters later. David and one of his men happened upon Saul, sound asleep and with his spear temptingly beside him. Again, David refused to do violence to the king:

> 'The Lord forbid that I should raise my hand against the Lord's anointed.'
> 1 SAMUEL 26:11 (NRSV)

So if you are considering assassinating your church leader – don't! I think it would be a fair use of these stories to say that such an action is forbidden. (You may possibly also draw that conclusion from the ten commandments!) But if your purpose is to call a leader to account – to make a truthful allegation of abusive behaviour – then you will find yourself lined up with many, many godly people in both the Old and New Testaments who did just that.

* * *

We'll look at a few examples. In the Old Testament, we might recall Nathan, who came to speak to David about his sexual impropriety with Bathsheba (2 Samuel 12).[51] Nathan explicitly called out David's abuse of power, likening him to a wealthy man who kills and eats his neighbour's pet lamb rather than slaughter one from his own herd. 'You are that man!' Nathan thundered against the king – an admirably brave thing to do, in those days of absolute monarchy.

You might also like to read the sarcastic words of the prophet Micaiah to Ahab, king of Israel (1 Kings 22:15–16), which exposed the king's thirst for battle, or the deeply scornful words of Elisha to King Jehoram of Israel, refusing to validate his kingship:

> Elisha said to the king of Israel, 'What have I to do with you? Go to your father's prophets or to your mother's… As the Lord of hosts lives, whom I serve, were it not that I have regard for King Jehoshaphat of Judah, I would give you neither a look nor a glance.'
> 2 KINGS 3:13–14 (NRSV)

There are so many other examples I could add. Calling the ancient kings to account isn't just tolerated by the Bible but actively encouraged. But let's move on to the New Testament.

Here, too, it is clear that *nobody* is above censure. In Galatians 2:6, we find the apostle Paul criticising Peter – and if any of the apostles could be said to be 'anointed', it would have to be Jesus' best friend, to whom the keys of the kingdom were given.

False teachers are condemned repeatedly in the New Testament letters. Peter has extremely fierce words against them:

> If they have escaped the corruption of the world by knowing our Lord and Saviour Jesus Christ and are again entangled in it and are overcome, they are worse off at the end than they were at the beginning. It would have been better for them not

to have known the way of righteousness, than to have known it and then to turn their backs on the sacred command that was passed on to them.

2 PETER 2:20–21

And how do we recognise a false teacher? Jesus (who had his own stern words for hypocritical religious leaders – see Matthew 23) said:

Watch out for false prophets. They come to you in sheep's clothing, but inwardly they are ferocious wolves. By their fruit you will recognise them. Do people pick grapes from thorn-bushes, or figs from thistles? Likewise, every good tree bears good fruit, but a bad tree bears bad fruit. A good tree cannot bear bad fruit, and a bad tree cannot bear good fruit. Every tree that does not bear good fruit is cut down and thrown into the fire. Thus, *by their fruit you will recognise them*.

MATTHEW 7:15–20 (my italics)

Touch not the Lord's anointed? If they are abusive and harming others, if they are bearing rotten fruit, it is our *duty* to call them out.

* * *

I'd like to finish this chapter by taking a look at the relatively obscure Old Testament book of Ezekiel. Ezekiel was a prophet, writing when the nation of Judah was in exile following their military defeat by Babylon. He had extremely strong words against the spiritual leaders of the nation who had failed the people so badly. It's worth reading the whole chapter (Ezekiel 34), but let me show you a couple of things.

The leaders (Ezekiel calls them shepherds) hadn't just been negligent or honestly mistaken. Rather than protecting the people (the sheep), they had actively preyed on them:

Woe to you shepherds of Israel who only take care of yourselves! Should not shepherds take care of the flock? You eat
the curds, clothe yourselves with the wool and slaughter the
choice animals, but you do not take care of the flock. You have
not strengthened the weak or healed those who are ill or bound
up the injured. You have not brought back the strays or searched
for the lost. You have ruled them harshly and brutally.

vv. 2–4

Ezekiel warms to his theme, reaching a damning conclusion:

As surely as I live, declares the Sovereign Lord, because my flock
lacks a shepherd and so has been plundered and has become
food for all the wild animals, and because my shepherds did not
search for my flock but cared for themselves rather than for my
flock, therefore, you shepherds, hear the word of the Lord: this
is what the Sovereign Lord says: *I am against the shepherds* and
will hold them accountable for my flock.

vv. 8–10 (my italics)

The false shepherds had placed themselves in opposition to God. This
is what every abusive church leader does: places himself in opposition to God.

* * *

But Ezekiel is not only charged with bringing words of judgement and
condemnation against the leaders. He also has words of comfort for
those they have harmed:

I myself will search for my sheep and look after them… I myself
will tend my sheep and make them lie down, declares the Sovereign Lord. I will search for the lost and bring back the strays.
I will bind up the injured and strengthen the weak.

vv. 11, 15–16

But God is also attentive to those *within the flock* who harm the weak:

> I will judge between one sheep and another, and between rams and goats. Is it not enough for you to feed on the good pasture? Must you also trample the rest of your pasture with your feet?… I myself will judge between the fat sheep and the lean sheep. Because you shove with flank and shoulder, butting all the weak sheep with your horns until you have driven them away, I will save my flock, and they will no longer be plundered. I will judge between one sheep and another.
>
> vv. 17–18, 20–22

God will not tolerate abusive leaders of God's people or the abuse of power between God's people. In the end, he will take matters into his own hands, judge abusers and care for those who are abused. 'I am the good shepherd,' said Jesus (John 10:11).

II

THE TRUTH WILL SET YOU FREE

In John 8, Jesus has a lengthy 'discussion' with the religious leaders about truth. (I put the word 'discussion' in quotation marks, because it reads more like an argument to me, at least as far as the religious leaders go.)

> To the Jews who had believed him, Jesus said, 'If you hold to my teaching, you are really my disciples. Then you will know the truth, and the truth will set you free.'
>
> They answered him, 'We are Abraham's descendants and have never been slaves of anyone. How can you say that we shall be set free?'
>
> Jesus replied, 'Very truly I tell you, everyone who sins is a slave to sin. Now a slave has no permanent place in the family, but a son belongs to it forever. So if the Son sets you free, you will be free indeed. I know you are Abraham's descendants. Yet you are looking for a way to kill me, because you have no room for my word. I am telling you what I have seen in the Father's presence, and you are doing what you have heard from your father.'
>
> 'Abraham is our father,' they answered.

'If you were Abraham's children,' said Jesus, 'then you would do what Abraham did. As it is, you are looking for a way to kill me, a man who has told you the truth that I heard from God. Abraham did not do such things. You are doing the works of your own father.'

'We are not illegitimate children,' they protested. 'The only Father we have is God himself.'

Jesus said to them, 'If God were your Father, you would love me, for I have come here from God. I have not come on my own; God sent me. Why is my language not clear to you? Because you are unable to hear what I say. You belong to your father, the devil, and you want to carry out your father's desires. He was a murderer from the beginning, not holding to the truth, for there is no truth in him. When he lies, he speaks his native language, for he is a liar and the father of lies. Yet because I tell the truth, you do not believe me! Can any of you prove me guilty of sin? If I am telling the truth, why don't you believe me? Whoever belongs to God hears what God says. The reason you do not hear is that you do not belong to God.'

JOHN 8:31–47

In a world where truth is often contested or viewed as irrelevant, Jesus' bold words here are refreshing, at least to those of us who follow him as master.

The gospel writer is very interested in truth. Here, he shows us Jesus as the one who speaks truth. Later on, he reveals Jesus as *the truth* (John 14:6). Truth, as John uses the word, is about God's view of reality, which is, of course, the true view of reality – 'I am telling you what I have seen in the Father's presence' (John 8:38); 'the truth that I heard from God' (v. 40). Truth is found in Jesus Christ and his word.

In contrast, those who oppose the truth were shown to have put themselves in opposition to God. They were spiritually incapable of discerning the truth (vv. 43, 47). They attempted to suppress the truth by argument, contradiction and intimidation. By the end of the chapter, the violence of their position is made clear: 'They picked up stones to stone him' (v. 59).

Now, please hear me right. I am *not* saying that anyone who interprets scripture differently from me is a devil. I am *not* saying that people in the churches who have unwittingly made life more difficult for women are suppressing the truth or are God's enemies.

But Jesus seems pretty clear that there *is* an enemy of God and humankind (however we visualise that being). And he, or it, demands the suppression of truth. The forces of evil would be keen to see scripture causing harm and not bringing blessing.

But truth? Truth is liberating. Truth will set us free.

Let's look at some of the scriptures that abusers don't want you to know about.

6

God is for the oppressed

I thought, 'God has forgotten me.'
Abuse survivor[52]

I don't know if an abuser has ever tried to make you think that God has forgotten you, or tried to convince you that God just doesn't care much about you. Or maybe things have just become so bad that it is hard for you to remember how much God cares about you. In this chapter I'm going to show you that God absolutely does care; he absolutely notices you; and he absolutely is on your side.

One of the things that abusers do is seize power. They gradually but systematically strip their wives of power. But powerlessness in the Bible is a cause for God's particular interest. He takes an interest in the affairs of us all, but he *particularly* takes an interest in those who are powerless.

To be honest, there are so many passages I could take you to that I'm spoilt for choice. I'm going to offer a few samples from various parts of the Bible to show you that it isn't a passing phase. God is *always* on the side of the powerless.

The Old Testament law

The Old Testament law has many, many places where God's concern for the poor, the widow, the victim and the outsider is revealed. Consider these verses from Leviticus 19:

Do not hold back the wages of a hired worker overnight.

Do not curse the deaf or put a stumbling-block in front of the blind...

Do not pervert justice; do not show partiality to the poor or favouritism to the great, but judge your neighbour fairly.

vv. 13–15

When a foreigner resides among you in your land, do not ill-treat them. The foreigner residing among you must be treated as your native-born...

Do not use dishonest standards when measuring length, weight or quantity. Use honest scales.

vv. 33–36

Or these beautiful laws from Deuteronomy 24, which assert human dignity:

When you make a loan of any kind to your neighbour, do not go into their house to get what is offered to you as a pledge. Stay outside and let the neighbour to whom you are making the loan bring the pledge out to you. If the neighbour is poor, do not go to sleep with their pledge in your possession. Return their cloak by sunset so that your neighbour may sleep in it. Then they will thank you...

Do not take advantage of a hired worker who is poor and needy, whether that worker is a fellow Israelite or a foreigner residing in one of your towns. Pay them their wages each day before sunset, because they are poor and are counting on it...

Do not deprive the foreigner or the fatherless of justice, or take the cloak of the widow as a pledge.

vv. 10–15, 17

When you are harvesting in your field and you overlook a sheaf, do not go back to get it. Leave it for the foreigner, the fatherless and the widow, so that the Lord your God may bless you in all the work of your hands. When you beat the olives from your trees, do not go over the branches a second time. Leave what remains for the foreigner, the fatherless and the widow. When you harvest the grapes in your vineyard, do not go over the vines again. Leave what remains for the foreigner, the fatherless and the widow.

vv. 19–21

I know that none of these is explicitly about domestic abuse, but they show us something of the heart of God for the dignity and protection of *everyone* in society.

The psalmists

The psalmists knew this. Their frequent appeals to God for vindication and for justice show that they believed he pays attention to the plight of the poor and the oppressed. Sometimes they assert that boldly:

'Because the poor are plundered and the needy groan,
    I will now arise,' says the Lord.
  'I will protect them from those who malign them.'
And the words of the Lord are flawless.

PSALM 12:5–6

Sometimes God's known heart for the oppressed forms the basis of a plea for God to act:

Have regard for your covenant,
    because haunts of violence fill the dark places of the land.
Do not let the oppressed retreat in disgrace;
    may the poor and needy praise your name.

PSALM 74:20–21

Concern for the poor forms the lynchpin of the prayer for the king in Psalm 72:

> Endow the king with your justice, O God,
>> the royal son with your righteousness.
> May he judge your people in righteousness,
>> your afflicted ones with justice…
> May he defend the afflicted among the people
>> and save the children of the needy;
>> may he crush the oppressor.
>
> vv. 1–2, 4

And then there is the beautiful cry for protection from violence, given in Psalm 140:

> Rescue me, Lord, from evildoers;
>> protect me from the violent,
> who devise evil plans in their hearts
>> and stir up war every day.
> They make their tongues as sharp as a serpent's;
>> the poison of vipers is on their lips.
> Keep me safe, Lord, from the hands of the wicked;
>> protect me from the violent,
>> who devise ways to trip my feet.
> The arrogant have hidden a snare for me;
>> they have spread out the cords of their net
>> and have set traps for me along my path.
> I say to the Lord, 'You are my God.'
>> Hear, Lord, my cry for mercy.
> Sovereign Lord, my strong deliverer,
>> you shield my head in the day of battle.
> Do not grant the wicked their desires, Lord;
>> do not let their plans succeed.
>
> vv. 1–8

The prophets

The prophets are equally convinced about the character of God and his heart for the oppressed. They express this in the form of angry polemics against abusers.

Amos is the most vocal of them. Against the injustice of the nations around, which includes people trafficking (1:6, 9), 'the Lord roars from Zion', he says (1:2). His words are even harsher against the nations of Israel and Judah, who ought to know better:

> This is what the Lord says:
> 'For three sins of Israel,
>   even for four, I will not relent.
> They sell the innocent for silver,
>   and the needy for a pair of sandals.
> They trample on the heads of the poor
>   as on the dust of the ground
>   and deny justice to the oppressed.
> Father and son use the same girl
>   and so profane my holy name.
> They lie down beside every altar
>   on garments taken in pledge.
> In the house of their god
>   they drink wine taken as fines...
> Now then, I will crush you
>   as a cart crushes when loaded with grain.
> The swift will not escape,
>   the strong will not muster their strength,
>   and the warrior will not save his life.'
>
> AMOS 2:6–8, 13–14

Amos has no doubts at all that God rages against the abuse of the vulnerable.

The rage of the Saviour

I wonder if you grew up knowing this children's rhyme. (It probably dates me, to be honest. I'll hastily say that I learned it at my mother's knee, and it was pretty outdated then.)

Gentle Jesus, meek and mild, look upon this little child.

Meek and mild? Well, Jesus most certainly didn't exhibit toxic masculinity, as we'll see in the next chapter. But he wasn't so meek and mild, either – not when it came to calling out the exploitation of the vulnerable.

You'll remember the story of the cleansing of the temple, I expect. It's in all four gospels (Matthew 21:12–17; Mark 11:15–19; Luke 19:45–48; John 2:13–25). Sometimes this story is told as though Jesus lost his temper, but nothing could be further from the truth. Jesus didn't lose his temper. He was not an unpredictable, violent man. But he did rage against those who would abuse the vulnerable.

In Mark's account (11:11), we learn that after the triumphal entry with the donkey and the palm leaves, Jesus went to the temple, had a look around and then went to stay with his friends for the night. It was the next day that he came back and cleared out the money-changers. This wasn't a loss of temper, but a staged event, an acted prophecy. (Just like the cursing of the fig tree, which wraps around the same story in Mark's gospel.)

Acted prophecy is one of the ways that the prophets communicated (for example, Jeremiah 13:1–11; Ezekiel 12:3–6). And although Jesus was more than a prophet, he certainly was a prophet.

So why did Jesus show himself to be so very much the opposite of meek and mild? Because God's house was being violated, and because women and non-Jews were unable to concentrate on their prayers because of the market trading. What got him riled up? Injustice.

There's another time that Jesus got angry. (I don't believe he lost his temper, but he was definitely angry.) And he used some pretty strong language. We read about this in Matthew 23. This time the target was the religious leaders: the people who were supposed to help the ordinary folk to learn about God and worship him. Instead, they were doing the opposite.

> Woe to you, teachers of the law and Pharisees, you hypocrites! You travel over land and sea to win a single convert, and when you have succeeded, you make them twice as much a child of hell as you are.
> MATTHEW 23:15

Jesus couldn't abide the idea that the religious leaders were blocking ordinary people's worship, that they were interfering with their encounter with God. What got him riled up? A form of injustice.

* * *

But the passage I really want us to focus on is a place where Jesus perhaps uses the strongest language of all:

> If any of you put a stumbling-block before one of these little ones who believe in me, it would be better for you if a great millstone were fastened around your neck and you were drowned in the depth of the sea. Woe to the world because of stumbling-blocks! Occasions for stumbling are bound to come, but woe to the one by whom the stumbling-block comes!
> MATTHEW 18:6-7 (NRSV)

Who are these 'little ones' of whom Jesus is so fiercely protective? Tom Wright summarises it beautifully:

> They include weak, vulnerable children, of course. But they also include those who are weak and vulnerable at other times of life, too: the cripples, the chronically sick, the elderly and infirm,

refugees, women (in many cultures), any who find themselves on the human scrap-heap that our world throws people on to when it can't think what else to do with them.[53]

Those who abuse the weak and vulnerable are under the judgement of God. And that is not a good place to be.

* * *

I don't know about you, but I *want* God to be angry about injustice and violence. I want a God who is not indifferent about it. I want a God who cares enough to rage against those who deliberately hurt and violate others.

And I want the Saviour that I follow to be like that, too. I'm glad he talks about millstones here – even though I quake at the possibility that I might be the cause of someone stumbling. I want Jesus to be angry with the perpetrator and tender to those who have been hurt.

Which is good, because he is.

But what about all that abuse against women in the Old Testament?

The Bible has some terrible stories of men sexually violating women. (If you're feeling strong, two of the worst examples are in Judges 19 and 2 Samuel 13. Otherwise, just take my word for it for now.) And sometimes people think this means that the Bible is saying men's violence towards women doesn't matter, that God's okay with it.

I don't believe this for one minute. And I hope I can persuade you, too.

Let's imagine the ancient world of our biblical writers. Undoubtedly in this ancient world, some men attacked women.

When a writer tells us stories about an ancient society, the way that God was working in history, he has a choice. Will he tell only male stories? Write the narrative as if it took place in a monastery or a boys' boarding school? Or will he include female stories?

If so, he will need to include stories of women being proactive and powerful, sometimes in a positive way and sometimes in a negative way. And if he is to represent the ancient society truthfully, he will need to include stories of women being acted upon, being subject to violence and abuse.

We know that the majority of the major players in the Old Testament are male. But there are some striking and powerful exceptions – both positive and negative. We meet Deborah and Jael, women of valour whom we mentioned briefly in chapter 2. And we meet Jezebel and Athaliah, powerful and scheming queens. Most of the Bible doesn't quite pass the Bechdel test[54] (the book of Ruth is an honourable exception), but nonetheless women do feature quite prominently in places.

But if the narrative is to be truthful, it must also portray the darker side of women's experience. If we did not find sexual violence portrayed, we would rightly be indignant that women's suffering was so irrelevant to the authors that they didn't bother to record it.

Of course, there are different ways of portraying sexual violence. It can be told at a discreet distance, or the reader can be brought up close like in a Quentin Tarantino film. In the narrated stories in which men rape women in the Old Testament, we are always kept at a discreet distance. There is no hint that the narrator is enjoying the story or inviting his readers to do so. This is not pornography.

More than this, though, the violation of women is treated very seriously by the Old Testament. The dreadful story in Judges 19 is a potent illustration of how low the nation of Israel had sunk. The story of Amnon raping Tamar in 2 Samuel 13 is a powerful critique of David's negligence as a father. And rapists often receive narrative comeuppance. Shechem is murdered by Dinah's brothers after he has violated her in Genesis 34, while Tamar's brother kills Amnon. The rapists of Judges 19 die in a civil war.

So these stories matter to the narrator. And the reason they matter is because women matter to God.

Why did God send Hagar back?

One of the stories I was challenged about by Jenny (see Introduction) is the story of Hagar. Why did God send Hagar back?

I agree that this is a troubling story, but there are some important things that we should notice, even here.

Let me recap the story in case you are unfamiliar with it. We referred to it briefly in chapter 1. The story begins in Genesis 16. Abraham has been waiting for the fulfilment of a promise made by God – a son. But he and his wife are old, and eventually Sarah his wife gets tired of waiting and gives her maidservant Hagar to Abraham to bear sons on her behalf. It's the story that inspired Margaret Atwood's *The Handmaid's Tale*.

But when Abraham impregnates Hagar, Sarah turns against her, making Hagar's life so miserable that she runs away into the desert. And it is there in the desert that she meets God, and God sends her back to Sarah and Abraham.

You can see why someone whose husband is abusing her would find this story troubling.

But there are some extraordinary features of Hagar's story that are often overlooked. In fact, Hagar is being treated with great respect by the narrator.

In Genesis 16, Hagar has fled to the desert because of the ill-treatment of her mistress. This is a desperate act – a desert is no place for a pregnant woman.

Here, in the desert, Hagar has an encounter with God so profound that she knows she is seen. She is not overlooked or forgotten by God. Her furtive, desperate flight into danger has been noted.

This is very surprising, if we stop to think about it. God is the god of Abraham her master and Sarah her mistress. By contrast, Hagar is Egyptian and would probably have retained some loyalty towards her own gods.

More than this, though, Hagar is a woman, a slave woman. A god wouldn't bother with the likes of her, would he?

But this God does care. He doesn't just speak to the wealthy man, Abraham. He also addresses Hagar, the Egyptian slave woman. He finds her in the desert (the 'angel of the Lord' is an Old Testament way of describing the appearance of God himself) and speaks words of strength to her.

True, he tells her to return home to her abusive mistress. (Given the alternative, going back was probably the safer option for a pregnant woman.) But he also makes her an astonishing promise, one that echoes the one he makes to Abraham. I've put them in parallel:

Hagar	Abraham
'I will so greatly multiply your offspring that they cannot be counted for multitude' (16:10, NRSV).	'[I] will make you exceedingly numerous… You shall be the ancestor of a multitude of nations' (Genesis 17:2, 4, NRSV).

Hagar, a matriarch! Who'd have seen that coming? She's travelled a long way since she was a mere slave who didn't even have rights over her own body.

Or perhaps we should put it another way. To Abraham and Sarah, Hagar will only ever be a slave woman with no rights. But to God, she is worthy not only of notice, but of God speaking to her and promising blessings to her. And he sees her with all the distinction and dignity of the matriarch she will become.

* * *

Hagar wants to celebrate this moment, to savour and remember it. So she does something unexpected. In the Old Testament, characters name places from time to time. Jacob will later name a place Beth-El (the house of God), because, as he says, 'Surely the Lord is in this place – and I did not know it!' (Genesis 28:16, NRSV). In a similar way, Abraham names a mountain:

> So Abraham called that place The Lord Will Provide. And to this day it is said, 'On the mountain of the Lord it will be provided.'
> GENESIS 22:14

But Hagar goes a step further than this – a huge step further. In order to mark this extraordinary encounter she has had with the God who unexpectedly sees and understands her, she gives God himself a name: El-Roi – the God who sees me.

In fact, she is the only character in the Bible who gives God a name.

* * *

There is another half to this story, and it involves Hagar having another encounter with God in the desert.

We wind forward a few years. Hagar's son Ishmael has been born, but Sarah, too, has had a son now (Isaac). And Sarah is concerned that the rights of her son should not be threatened by this older boy in whom she has now lost interest. So Sarah sends Hagar and Ishmael away into the desert with the full knowledge and connivance of Abraham.

Now things get pretty interesting, because Hagar's story is told in a way that parallels Abraham's, in particular with the story of the near-sacrifice of Isaac. In both accounts, the parent is setting off with their child into a situation from which they are sure their child will not return alive.[55]

Hagar and Ishmael (Genesis 21)	**Abraham and Isaac (Genesis 22)**
There is a solemn journey and a send-off with insufficient provisions (bread and a skin of water), signifying the child's short life expectancy (v. 14).	There is a solemn journey and a send-off with wood, fire and knife, signifying the child's short life expectancy (vv. 3, 6).
An angel calls from heaven to rescue Ishmael (vv. 17–18).	An angel calls from heaven to rescue Isaac (vv. 11–12).
God opens Hagar's eyes and she sees the means of her son's salvation – a well (v. 19).	God opens Abraham's eyes and he sees the means of his son's salvation – a ram (v. 13).
Her child is saved to become a great nation (v. 18).	His child is saved to become a great nation (vv. 16–17).

This is not a coincidence. These ancient writers are far too skilful and subtle for these parallels to be accidental. On the contrary, the parallels have been put there under the Spirit's inspiration to show us something stunning.

Hagar – the foreign slave woman, who has no rights over her own body, whose home situation is abusive and dangerous – is viewed by God with as much dignity and value as the great Abraham himself.

Rightly did she name him 'the God who sees me', because God is always taking note of the treatment of those who have been abused.

7

Jesus: fellow sufferer and non-toxic man

Does God really understand?

Abuse survivor[56]

The incarnation of God

If you've been around church for a while (and even if you haven't), you'll almost certainly know the wonderful Christmas carol 'Hark! The herald angels sing'. Carols vary in the depth of their theology ('The holly and the ivy'?), but this one is a particularly rich one, in my opinion.

The second verse reads like this:

> *Christ, by highest heaven adored,*
> *Christ, the everlasting Lord;*
> *late in time behold him come,*
> *offspring of a virgin's womb.*
> *Veiled in flesh the Godhead see,*
> *hail the incarnate deity;*
> *pleased as man with man to dwell,*
> *Jesus, our Emmanuel.*

Charles Wesley, the hymn-writer, is exploring the great mystery and wonder of the incarnation – God-in-flesh.

The enfleshment of God is one of the most precious things the Bible tells us about. God is not like a watchmaker who has wound the universe up and leaves it to slowly wind down. He is not on the outside looking into a closed system, like a child watching a snow globe.

The Old Testament describes God's relationship with his people in many different ways, but it is probably fair to say that before Jesus the way God related to people was by occasional intervention. Though engaged with the world, God was still, in some sense, distant from it.

But one day it all changed.

Enter a baby, crying in a manger. A small child being toilet-trained. A young man learning the craft of carpentry, with cuts and bruises to prove it. Now we have God with dirty hands. A God who understands what it means to have sore feet at the end of the day, a tired back from physical labour. A God who has felt the sun on his face in the morning and enjoyed his supper in the evening. A God who understands.

There are four things in particular that I'd like to show you that Jesus understands.

Jesus was misunderstood

The gospel accounts are full of people misunderstanding Jesus and failing to believe him. He wasn't even acknowledged in his home town (Mark 6:1–6). In particular, his own family disbelieved him (John 7:1–5) and at times thought that he was mad:

> Then Jesus entered a house, and again a crowd gathered, so that he and his disciples were not even able to eat. When his family heard about this, they went to take charge of him, for they said, 'He is out of his mind.'
> MARK 3:20–21

Jesus' friends, too, misunderstood him regularly. On one occasion we get a glimpse of Jesus' disappointment and perhaps frustration:

> Don't you know me, Philip, even after I have been among you such a long time?
> JOHN 14:9

Sometimes it wasn't just clumsiness but wilful misunderstanding, such as the time that the Pharisees accused him of being in league with the devil:

> Then they brought him a demon-possessed man who was blind and mute, and Jesus healed him, so that he could both talk and see. All the people were astonished and said, 'Could this be the Son of David?'
> But when the Pharisees heard this, they said, 'It is only by Beelzebul, the prince of demons, that this fellow drives out demons.'
> MATTHEW 12:22–24

Jesus knew what it was to be lied about, considered mad and misunderstood. Perhaps you live with similar hurt? Jesus understands.

Jesus was betrayed

In chapter 4 we looked at Psalm 55, a psalm written by someone who had been betrayed by someone they trusted.

Jesus was betrayed to his death by a friend, someone he'd spent three years with, who had had a trusted position within the group of disciples. The incident is recorded in all four gospels. Here, John tells us of what happened immediately after Jesus washed his disciples' feet:

> Jesus was troubled in spirit and testified, 'Very truly I tell you, one of you is going to betray me… It is the one to whom I will give this piece of bread when I have dipped it in the dish.' Then,

dipping the piece of bread, he gave it to Judas, the son of Simon Iscariot. As soon as Judas took the bread, Satan entered into him.

So Jesus told him, 'What you are about to do, do quickly.' But no one at the meal understood why Jesus said this to him. Since Judas had charge of the money, some thought Jesus was telling him to buy what was needed for the festival, or to give something to the poor. As soon as Judas had taken the bread, he went out. And it was night.

JOHN 13:21, 26–30

Jesus knew what it was to be betrayed by someone he should have been able to trust and rely on. Perhaps you live with similar hurt? Jesus understands.

Jesus experienced physical abuse

Years ago, I was privileged to visit Israel–Palestine. One of the most memorable moments for me was retracing Jesus' steps from the garden of Gethsemane, where he was arrested, down into the Kidron Valley and up into the city of Jerusalem. Inside the city we visited a recently excavated house, which is thought to have belonged to Caiaphas the high priest. Beneath that house there was a small windowless room that would have served as a dungeon. Nowadays, it has a set of stairs to provide access, but they are modern. Once, the only access would have been by lowering the prisoner through a hole in the ceiling.

If that truly was Caiaphas' house, then we know Jesus was taken there the night he was betrayed (Matthew 26:57–75). And though the gospels don't make it clear where Jesus was detained overnight, it seems quite possible that it was in this dungeon. For me, standing in that place provided an opportunity to imagine, just for a moment, how Jesus might have felt, awaiting his torture and execution the following morning. I found it incredibly moving.

Before his crucifixion, Jesus experienced physical beating and other forms of torture. The Romans knew how to make a scourge that would flay a person. Fit men died under such treatment. I won't go into details, but if you've seen Mel Gibson's *The Passion of the Christ*, you may have some idea. Suffice it to say that the relatively bald gospel accounts conceal a world of pain. He was beaten at least twice:

> Then the high priest tore his clothes and said, 'He has spoken blasphemy! Why do we need any more witnesses? Look, now you have heard the blasphemy. What do you think?'
>
> 'He is worthy of death,' they answered.
>
> Then they spat in his face and struck him with their fists. Others slapped him and said, 'Prophesy to us, Messiah. Who hit you?'
>
> MATTHEW 26:65–68

> Then Pilate took Jesus and had him flogged. The soldiers twisted together a crown of thorns and put it on his head. They clothed him in a purple robe and went up to him again and again, saying, 'Hail, king of the Jews!' And they slapped him in the face.
>
> JOHN 19:1–3

And then came the agony of crucifixion, which Mark tells us lasted from nine o'clock in the morning until three in the afternoon (Mark 15:25, 33–34).

Jesus knew what it was to be physically abused. Perhaps you live with similar hurt? Jesus understands.

Jesus experienced nakedness and humiliation

It is perhaps only in the past few years that the stripping of Jesus became a focus of attention, when David Tombs showed us what we should have seen all along:

After being condemned by Pilate, the guards took Jesus into the governor's headquarters. In front of 'the whole cohort', that likely numbered over five hundred soldiers, the guards 'stripped him and put a scarlet robe on him' (Mt. 27:28). He was mocked, beaten and spat upon by a crowd of soldiers before being stripped again according to Mark 15:20 and Matthew 27:31. Based on what the Gospels affirm, Jesus was first stripped naked to be flogged. The soldiers then stripped him again and dressed him for his journey through the city. They then stripped him once more and exhibited him naked on the cross until he died before a mocking crowd… For both the Romans and the Jews, nakedness during execution was a sign of humiliation and absolute powerlessness in which shame and dishonour were integral factors in the punishment.[57]

The gospels do not tell us that Jesus was sexually assaulted, though it is quite possible. But he was certainly humiliated with nakedness.

Perhaps you live with similar hurt? Jesus understands.

* * *

One of the titles given to Jesus is Emmanuel, which means 'God with us'. And so we can sing:

> *Veiled in flesh the Godhead see,*
> *hail the incarnate deity;*
> *pleased as man with man to dwell,*
> *Jesus, our Emmanuel.*

But there is another element to the incarnation of Jesus that I'd like to draw your attention to – how he related to women.

Jesus honoured women

Perhaps it is no wonder that women were first at the cradle and last at the cross. They had never known a man like this man. There never has been such another. A prophet and teacher who never nagged them, never flattered or coaxed or patronized; who never made sick jokes about women; who rebuked without querulousness and praised without condescension; who took women's questions and arguments seriously; who never mapped out a certain sphere for women; who never urged them to be feminine or jeered at them for being female; who had no axe to grind and no uneasy male dignity to defend; who took women as he found them and was completely unselfconscious. There is no act, no sermon, no parable in the whole Gospel that borrows its point or pungency from female perversity. Nobody could get from the words and deeds of Jesus that there was anything funny or inferior about women.[58]

The brilliant Dorothy L. Sayers nails it here. Jesus is the absolute opposite of toxic masculinity. In this section I am going to remind you of four encounters that Jesus had with women.

The bleeding woman (Mark 5:21–43; Luke 8:40–56)

It was a busy day for Jesus. He had crossed the lake in his friends' boat to be met by a great crowd clamouring for his attention. He had been healing and teaching, and then he had urgently been summoned to the bedside of a dying child, Jairus' daughter. Jesus was making his way through the press of people when suddenly he stopped. Power had gone out of him without his authorisation – it had been 'stolen', as it were.

The disciples were confused. How could Jesus distinguish one person's touch from another's? The crowd was pressing around him densely. Many hands were upon him.

And, we imagine, Jairus was desperate. I envisage him hopping about on the periphery, hoping to catch Jesus' eye and attention once more: 'Come on! This is urgent!'

But Jesus wasn't to be hurried. He wanted to identify the person who had touched him in faith. Then, out of the crowd crept a woman. Exposure was just what she had hoped to avoid – because she had a shameful secret.

Twelve years ago she had starting bleeding. She probably thought it was a normal period at first, but it never stopped.

Nowadays there is medical treatment that we could try. We might go on the pill, get a D&C or perhaps a hysterectomy. Of course, no such options were available to the woman. But she had tried – Luke tells us she had spent all her money on physicians.

And she had good reason to try. Her constant bleeding wasn't just making her anaemic and weak; it also made her ritually unclean. As Leviticus tells us:

> When a woman has a discharge of blood for many days at a time other than her monthly period or has a discharge that continues beyond her period, she will be unclean as long as she has the discharge, just as in the days of her period.
> LEVITICUS 15:25

And that uncleanness would be transmitted to anything or anyone she touched:

> Any bed she lies on while her discharge continues will be unclean, as is her bed during her monthly period, and anything she sits on will be unclean, as during her period. Anyone who touches them will be unclean; they must wash their clothes and bathe with water, and they will be unclean till evening.
> vv. 26–27

This meant, if she were obedient to the law, that she couldn't cook food for her family. She couldn't have sex with her husband. She shouldn't even live with other people. She most certainly shouldn't have been out and about in a crowd, contaminating everyone she touched. And how *dare* she touch a holy man!

But Jesus was not shocked, and he wasn't repulsed by her 'women's trouble'. Instead, he looked on her with love and compassion. He didn't patronise; he didn't criticise. He simply praised her faith and assured her of healing:

> He said to her, 'Daughter, your faith has healed you. Go in peace and be freed from your suffering.'
> MARK 5:34

The adulteress (John 8:1–11)

> The teachers of the law and the Pharisees brought in a woman caught in adultery. They made her stand before the group and said to Jesus, 'Teacher, this woman was caught in the act of adultery.'
> JOHN 8:3–4

How do you catch a couple in flagrante? I guess it could have been an accident. Maybe the couple were incautious and someone stumbled across them. What a 'happy' coincidence that Jesus was in town at the time. Much more likely, I think, is that the scribes and Pharisees had been watching this couple for a while, having realised that they would provide an excellent pretext to trap Jesus. And so, at just the right moment, they burst in, surprising them in the very act. Nice.

Somehow, the man had slipped through their fingers, though. Surprise! I wonder how he managed that. Was he one of them, perhaps? Or maybe they just weren't interested in bringing a man to judgement. The woman made a much sorrier picture.

What was she wearing, I wonder? Just a bedsheet? The scribes and Pharisees carried on:

> 'In the Law Moses commanded us to stone such women. Now what do you say?' They were using this question as a trap, in order to have a basis for accusing him.
>   *But Jesus bent down and started to write on the ground with his finger.* When they kept on questioning him, he straightened up and said to them, 'Let any one of you who is without sin be the first to throw a stone at her.' *Again he stooped down and wrote on the ground.*
> vv. 5–8 (my italics)

People have speculated for centuries about what Jesus was writing in the dust. He certainly seemed very intent upon it. Was he writing the law, as the finger of God wrote it on the stone tablets for Moses? Was he writing the names of the woman's accusers?

I reckon I know – though of course I can't prove it to you, and I may be wrong. But this is my theory.

Jesus was averting his eyes.

Imagine the woman's experience. The circle of leering men around her, eager to crush her body with stones, to carve their hate into her flesh. And written across her face, the shame, the regret, the fear. At that moment the most powerful thing that any man could do would be to refuse to look at her. He was not embarrassed by her; but in order to respect her, to honour the value that no one else saw within her, he averted his eyes.

In Mark 10:21, we are told that Jesus looked at the rich young ruler and loved him. But in this moment, the act of love was to look away.

> At this, those who heard began to go away one at a time, the older ones first, until only Jesus was left, with the woman still

standing there. Jesus straightened up and asked her, 'Woman, where are they? Has no one condemned you?'

'No one, sir,' she said.

'Then neither do I condemn you,' Jesus declared. 'Go now and leave your life of sin.'

vv. 9–11

Brilliant, as always. (I love Jesus for his brilliance and wit as well as for his many other qualities.) Who is ashamed by the end of this story? The accusers.

And to the woman, the word of grace and truth: *I do not condemn you. From now on sin no more.*

The Samaritan woman (John 4:1–42)

There are several stories in the Old Testament in which couples meet at a well and then get married – think of Isaac, Jacob and Moses. So for the original readers of this story in John's gospel, all sorts of possibilities might be in their minds.

The disciples had gone off to buy food and the villagers were resting out of the midday sun. Horrors – a man and a woman alone together! It gets worse and worse!

And she's clearly a Very Bad Woman. Or so many commentators have told us. More on that in a moment.

One thing is certain – life hasn't been easy for her. Married five times already, she is now living with a sixth man, who is not her husband.

I wonder how much say she had in any of those marriages. I wonder how much say she had in any of her divorces. (If divorced she was – the gospel says nothing about whether she had been widowed or put aside.)

The answer to both questions is that she probably had very little say. Women tended not to in those days.

And I wonder why she is now living in an informal arrangement. Here's an alternative possibility.

Maybe she wasn't a serial adulteress, as some people have creatively imagined. Maybe she wasn't a Very Bad Woman at all. Maybe she needed to provide for her children or herself and would rather cohabit than become a prostitute. (What other options would be available to her if no man would marry her?)

But, whatever her background, here's the danger. This woman was a prime candidate for a man to take advantage of. Like this:

> The disruption of my life began at age 14... For months, my youth minister had showered me with flattering attention, telling me that God had chosen me to help his ministry. This grooming led to 18 months of progressively worse sexual abuse, layered with threats. When I could not tolerate the abuse any longer, I told the only person whom I thought could stop it – my pastor... My pastor's response was to fire the youth minister and pick up with me where the youth minister had left off.
> Abuse survivor[59]

I wonder what the Samaritan woman thought as she saw the man sitting beside her well. She needed to go there for water. There were probably no alternatives. There was no one within earshot. And in any case, if she were to be raped, they'd probably only blame her. Because she was That Sort of Woman.

I'm reminded of another terrible modern event, when men in Rotherham systematically abused girls, and this was ignored by the authorities for far too long because they were That Sort of Girl.

If she seems a little prickly with Jesus, might that not be the reason?

But this man wants nothing more from her than a cup of water. And – miraculously – what he has to offer her (living water) has no strings or agendas.

She is a woman who has been 'known' many times. But here is a man who knows her intimately but does not objectify her; he sees her history and loves her purely. He doesn't leer; he doesn't make innuendos; he doesn't make smutty jokes afterwards with his mates. His private conduct is wholly in line with his public appearance.

She is safer with him than she could be anywhere else on earth.

The forgiven sinner (Luke 7:36–50)

Not that Jesus always avoided scandal.

> When one of the Pharisees invited Jesus to have dinner with him, he went to the Pharisee's house and reclined at the table. A woman in that town who lived a sinful life learned that Jesus was eating at the Pharisee's house, so she came there with an alabaster jar of perfume. As she stood behind him at his feet weeping, she began to wet his feet with her tears. Then she wiped them with her hair, kissed them and poured perfume on them.
>
> Luke 7:36–38

Here he is at dinner in the house of a Pharisee. What possessed this woman to choose this moment to express her love for Jesus? Maybe he was heading out of town the next day, and she knew she needed to seize her opportunity.

So there is Jesus, reclining at the table with his disciples and his host and probably some other Pharisees too. Life was fairly public in those days, so the entrance of other people during the meal isn't itself surprising.

But what the woman did was positively scandalous.

First, it was scandalously extravagant, which would have invited impertinent speculation about the nature of their previous relationship.

But that is nothing compared to her next actions. Massaging his feet, weeping over him, drying her feet with her loosened hair – even to modern readers that sounds remarkably suggestive. I think Simon the Pharisee and his friends were apoplectic.

Didn't Jesus know that this was a 'sinner'?

Of course Jesus knew. And once again he refused to take advantage of a vulnerable woman. Once again he was a safe person to be with. Once again he spoke words of love and dignity:

> 'Do you see this woman? I came into your house. You did not give me any water for my feet, but she wet my feet with her tears and wiped them with her hair. You did not give me a kiss, but this woman, from the time I entered, has not stopped kissing my feet. You did not put oil on my head, but she has poured perfume on my feet. Therefore, I tell you, her many sins have been forgiven – as her great love has shown. But whoever has been forgiven little loves little.'
> Then Jesus said to her, 'Your sins are forgiven… Your faith has saved you; go in peace.'
> vv. 44–48, 50

For the self-satisfied (men) in the room: words of criticism. And for the vulnerable (woman): love, compassion and dignity.

No, there was nothing about Jesus that could be described as toxic masculinity.

8

You are of immense value

He constantly belittled me. He told me I was ugly, stupid, a bad mother.
Abuse survivor[60]

In her brilliant book on domestic abuse, *Out of Control* (which I highly recommend), Natalie Collins lists eight classic abuse tactics. Very briefly, they are: isolating, humiliating, threatening, exhausting, brainwashing (also known as gaslighting), use of overt violence, making demands and love-bombing (use of extreme flattery, excessive gifts and so on). All of these tactics are ways of the abuser achieving and maintaining control. It is striking how many of them involve belittling and humiliating her. For example, Collins writes:

> The Humiliator might compare his partner unfavourably to other women, sexually or otherwise, pointing out how other women are better wives, lovers, mothers. He tells her they are prettier, sexier, kinder, thinner, more intellectual, less annoying… He makes her beg for his love or forgiveness, possibly using Bible passages to justify himself. Calling her a Jezebel, he tells her she is sinful like Eve.[61]

But what an abuser will not tell you is that the Bible is enormously positive about your value, your dignity and your worth. Let's have a look at what the Bible actually says.

You are made in the image of God

We've already looked at some of the ways in which Genesis 1—3 might have been weaponised against you. In this section I want us to consider one of the wonderful, positive things that it says – something you should revel in and take to heart.

> Then God said, 'Let us make man in our image, after our likeness. And let them have dominion over the fish of the sea and over the birds of the heavens and over the livestock and over all the earth and over every creeping thing that creeps on the earth.'
>   So God created man in his own image,
>   in the image of God he created him;
>   male and female he created them.
>   And God blessed them.
> GENESIS 1:26–28 (ESV)

Perhaps you are thinking, 'That's all about men – how does it show my value as a woman?'

If you read this in some more modern or looser translations (e.g. the New Living Translation or the Good News Translation), it will speak of God making 'human beings' rather than 'man'. I've deliberately kept the 'man' language here so we can see that, even in this more literal form, it does not exclude women. In other words, it's not just modern versions smoothing it out for us – we women were in the mind of the author (and therefore of God) all along. Let me show you how.

* * *

There are a couple of clues that tell us that women are absolutely included here. First, the word translated 'man' is *adam* (which later is used as a personal name – Adam). The best translation of this word is 'human'. There is a very common Hebrew word for a male human (*ish*), and if our writer had wanted to indicate that only males are being referred to, he could have used this word instead.

The second thing to notice is the poetic structure that is being used. Hebrew poetry uses a form called 'parallelism'. If you've spent much time reading the Psalms, you'll have noticed it. In the most common form of parallelism, the two half-lines say more or less the same thing twice. For example, in Psalm 51:4, the writer says of God:

| You are right | in your verdict |
| and [you are] justified | when you judge |

The two halves of the verse mirror one another. We might loosely say that

You are right = you are justified

and

in your verdict = when you judge.

In a similar way, we have a parallelism in the Genesis verses we looked at earlier:

| In the image of God | he created | him; |
| Male and female | he created | them. |

By the same logic, we see that the poet is matching 'male and female' with the 'image of God'. God created humankind in his image: both male *and* female. Neither sex has the monopoly on being image-bearers.

* * *

What is this 'image of God' all about?

It is a beautiful, rich idea – far bigger and deeper and lovelier than most people realise.

In the ancient world, when this was written, 'image of God' would have reminded the people of an idol in a temple. In those days, *every* pagan temple had the statue of its god inside. The people believed that the god would act through the idol. His image didn't just represent him, but it somehow mediated the god's power.

But the Hebrew temple did not have an idol. In fact, the making of idols was strictly forbidden in the ten commandments. Why?

Because God was *already represented* within the great temple of the universe – by Adam and Eve. By male and female, made in his image. By you and me. No carved statue can come close to us as the living, breathing representatives of his glory and mediators of his blessing. This is saying something incredible about the value and dignity of human life, female and male.

Sisters, we are made in the image of God. We are living, breathing representatives of his glory and mediators of his blessing to the world.

* * *

The other idea which the ancient audience would think of when they heard 'image' is a king setting up a statue. You can go to the British Museum, or to a hundred other places around the world, and find carved statues of kings. Just think of the great Egyptian statues of the pharaohs. Kings (and queens) have always replicated their image – they still do today. Statues, coins, stamps, paintings – it's a way of asserting their authority. Where the statue stood, the king governed. It represented his royal sovereignty.

In a similar way, the human vocation to be the image of God is about our bringing God's authority to bear. It is about our ruling the world as God's vice-regents.

This is our purpose as humans, our vocation: to do God's work in the world, to represent God to the world and to govern the world with divine authority and in God's good way. Yes, the role of governance is given to both men and women. Note again the plural language of verse 26:

Let *them* have dominion.

That includes you and me, sisters. An abuser doesn't want you to know this, but God does.

* * *

As Lucy Peppiatt says in *Rediscovering Scripture's Vision for Women* (another book you should definitely have on your bookshelf):

If man and woman have their origins in the being of God, then woman is not other to God but *intrinsically connected* to his being and image.[62]

God's heart is to bind your wounds and restore your dignity

There's one more cluster of passages that I'd like to draw your attention to at this point. We begin with the book of the prophet Isaiah, the continuation of the passage Jesus read at the synagogue in Nazareth when he was setting out the manifesto for his ministry:

The Spirit of the Sovereign Lord is on me,
      because the Lord has anointed me
      to proclaim good news to the poor.
He has sent me to bind up the broken-hearted,
      to proclaim freedom for the captives
      and release from darkness for the prisoners,
to proclaim the year of the Lord's favour
      and the day of vengeance of our God...
ISAIAH 61:1–2

The prophet is speaking about the 'job description' of the faithful servant of God – a role, of course, perfectly filled by Jesus (though when Jesus read it aloud, he omitted the last of the lines above). This job description is all about healing and restoration: recovery of sight for the blind and freedom for the oppressed. It's a wonderful statement of God's purposes for us – his purposes of blessing.

But the prophet continues, and the next part is equally beautiful, though less well-known:

> … to comfort all who mourn,
>   and provide for those who grieve in Zion –
> to bestow on them a crown of beauty
>   instead of ashes,
> the oil of joy
>   instead of mourning,
> and a garment of praise
>   instead of a spirit of despair.
> They will be called oaks of righteousness,
>   a planting of the Lord
>   for the display of his splendour.
>
> ISAIAH 61:2–3

Now, in the original context, these words are addressed to Judah, a nation that has been ravaged by war. The book of Lamentations describes the nation's suffering in powerful, first-person, *female* poetry:

> How lonely sits the city
>   that once was full of people!
> How like a widow she has become,
>   she that was great among the nations…
> She weeps bitterly in the night,
>   with tears on her cheeks.
>
> LAMENTATIONS 1:1–2 (NRSV)

And then, in the most extraordinary, tender language, the Lamenter goes on to grieve for the violation of the city, which he describes in terms of sexual violence and utter desolation:

> Enemies have stretched out their hands
>   over all her precious things;
> she has even seen the nations
>   invade her sanctuary...
> Is it nothing to you, all you who pass by?
>   Look and see
> if there is any sorrow like my sorrow...
> The Lord handed me over
>   to those whom I cannot withstand...
> The Lord has trodden as in a wine press
>   the virgin daughter Judah...
> For these things I weep;
>   my eyes flow with tears...
> Zion stretches out her hands,
>   but there is no one to comfort her.
> LAMENTATIONS 1:10, 12, 14–17 (NRSV)

It is to this violated people, into this situation of utter desolation, that Isaiah speaks the divine words of comfort:

> Comfort, comfort my people,
>   says your God.
> Speak tenderly to Jerusalem.
> ISAIAH 40:1–2

And the comfort is still being expressed in Isaiah 61, in the words we just read:

> ... to comfort all who mourn,
>   and provide for those who grieve in Zion –
> to bestow on them a crown of beauty
>   instead of ashes,

> the oil of joy
>> instead of mourning.

This is the mission of the servant of God. It was Jesus' mission; it is the church's mission. And it expresses God's love and tenderness to the bruised and the broken, the violated and the victimised.

But Isaiah is not done yet. The prophet warms to his theme. (Really, I'm struggling to choose which excerpts to share with you – it's all wonderful!) In the next chapter, we read these words:

> The nations will see your vindication,
>> and all kings your glory;
> you will be called by a new name
>> that the mouth of the Lord will bestow.
> You will be a crown of splendour in the Lord's hand,
>> a royal diadem in the hand of your God.
> No longer will they call you Deserted,
>> or name your land Desolate.
> But you will be called Hephzibah ['my delight is in her'],
> and your land Beulah ['married'];
> for the Lord will take delight in you,
>> and your land will be married.
> As a young man marries a young woman,
>> so will your Builder marry you;
> as a bridegroom rejoices over his bride,
>> so will your God rejoice over you.
> ISAIAH 62:2–5

This does not exclude men. But do not forget this: Jerusalem was visualised as a woman who had been broken and raped, whom God tenderly restored, bound up and rejoiced over like a bride – a royal diadem in the hand of God.

This is what God desires for you.

But what about sin?

In this chapter, we have looked at female dignity and value in the sight of God. But you might have doubts about this. You might be thinking: What about sin? What about my brokenness? What about all the times I've let God, or other people, down? Aren't I just a… [*insert whatever horrible word the abuser has called you*]?

Let's take a look at this.

The Bible tells us that we are all sinners. You know that, I guess. That's why we need a Saviour. But there are four things I'd like to show you from the Bible.

Not all sin is the same

Most of us have been told this from time to time: 'All sin is equally black before God.' Maybe your abuser has told you this, to minimise his crimes and maximise any wrongs you have done.

It's just not true.

Yes, the Bible tells us that before the holiness of God we are all sinners. We are all in need of the saving work of Jesus Christ. But does it say that all sin is equal? Absolutely not.

Take Jesus' comments about the sin against the Holy Spirit (Mark 3:22–30). This is clearly much worse than other sins. Or take Paul's self-description as 'the worst' of sinners (1 Timothy 1:15). How could he be chief among sinners if all sin is the same? The apostle John divides sins into those that 'lead to death' and those that don't (1 John 5:16–17).

If you want more evidence, look at the way that Jesus rages against the abuse of 'little ones' (Matthew 18:6–7) or his fury at the Pharisees who 'shut the door of the kingdom of heaven in people's faces' (Matthew 23:13). Compare these with the gentle way he addressed the woman taken in adultery: 'Neither do I condemn you... Go now and leave your life of sin' (John 8:11).

Some sins are worse than others, and causing harm to the vulnerable is up there in the top rank.

You are forgiven

Perhaps the biblical truth about universal sinfulness has been used to make you feel worthless. Perhaps the abuser has used it to taunt you, to humiliate you and to diminish you. Perhaps he has dredged up things from the past that you wish could be forgotten. If that is your situation, know this: if you are a Christian, *God has utterly forgiven you*.

Corrie ten Boom was a woman who knew a bit about forgiveness. (Her book *The Hiding Place* is the extraordinary story of her family's courageous faithfulness to God during the Nazi occupation of Holland.) She said this:

> When we confess our sins, God casts them into the deepest ocean, gone forever... God then places a sign out there that says, 'NO FISHING'.[63]

She's absolutely right. The apostle Paul says the same thing, using the metaphor of a courtroom:

> There is therefore now no condemnation for those who are in Christ Jesus... If God is for us, who is against us?... Who will bring any charge against God's elect? It is God who justifies. Who is to condemn?
>
> ROMANS 8:1, 31, 33–34 (NRSV)

If God has declared you forgiven, *nobody* has the right to condemn you. Nobody has the right to contradict God.

And, if you are reading this and wondering if this forgiveness and grace could apply to you, the answer is yes! Could *you* be included in that massive ocean of God's grace and forgiveness? Most certainly. If you have never put yourself into the loving hands of God, he is holding them out to you today. You don't need to be good enough. You don't need to *be* anything. Jesus said:

> Whoever comes to me I will never drive away.
> JOHN 6:37

Jesus died for you

For those with low self-esteem and those who have been systematically blamed and ridiculed, even this wonderful truth could feel heavy. 'Jesus died for me. Does that mean I am responsible for Jesus' death?' Is this something else to blame ourselves for?

The Bible never uses this as a stick to beat us with. Anyone who says, 'Your sins were so bad that they killed Jesus,' is misusing scripture and forgetting their own sinfulness.

It is just the opposite. Jesus' willing death is a reflection of his love for you and of your value in his sight. Jesus said:

> God loved the world *so much* that he gave his only Son.
> JOHN 3:16 (GNT, my italics)

> Greater love has no one than this: to lay down one's life for one's friends.
> JOHN 15:13

If you still doubt that you are precious to God, I hope that the willing death of Jesus to make you part of his family can persuade you that you are indeed loved by God.

The cross is the remedy for it all

While we're on the subject of the cross, I'm going to touch very briefly on something that has inspired millions of pages of writing. Here, I'm going to give it just a few lines.

The cross is the remedy for your sin and for my sin. We looked at that a few moments ago. But the cross is also sometimes described as a battle victory. Do you remember this passage in Colossians?

> God made you alive with Christ. He forgave us all our sins, having cancelled the charge of our legal indebtedness, which stood against us and condemned us; he has taken it away, nailing it to the cross. And having disarmed the powers and authorities, he made a public spectacle of them, triumphing over them by the cross.
>
> COLOSSIANS 2:13–15

The language of 'powers and authorities' that Paul uses here refers to spiritual forces that seek to cause harm and disruption. While there is much debate about the idea of a 'personal devil', it's not hard to believe that evil exists – that there are forces, powers and structures that cause and perpetuate dreadful things.

They are defeated at the cross.

* * *

The cross provides the remedy for it all.

It's not just about your forgiveness. It's about your healing, too.

It's not just about what you have done. It's about what has been done to you.

It all finds its healing at the cross.

At the cross, the forces of evil find themselves under judgement. They are condemned. At the cross they are defeated. They are paraded in humiliation, the way that a conquering Roman general would parade his conquered enemies through the streets of Rome. Oh, I wish we could see the full outworking of that right now, and we are not told why God makes us wait. But it is still true. Here, in the willing self-sacrifice of the Son of God, is the healing for all the pain of the world. For all *your* pain.

The cross is a measure of how much God loves you, and it is a measure of what lengths he will go to in order to eradicate the forces of evil.

Because you are so very precious in his sight.

9

Silenced and hidden no more

I knew the violence against me wasn't right, but the Bible was being used to prevent me from calling it out... I became the problem in the church's eyes.

Abuse survivor, interview transcript

There was a culture of silence, a culture of submission. There was no context to resist or complain.

Abuse survivor, interview transcript

In October 2017, allegations about film producer Harvey Weinstein suddenly started to come out. As one well-known female celebrity after another described him abusing them, a hashtag emerged on social media: #MeToo.

#MeToo had been posted on Twitter 500,000 times by 16 October 2017. On Facebook, the hashtag was used by more than 4.7 million people during the first 24 hours.

It felt as if a tipping point was being reached. Suddenly women (and some men) in all walks of life were able to express what had been done to them. Suddenly the dark undercurrents of sexual assault and abuse running below the surface in many industries, departments and – yes – churches were being brought into the light.

#MeToo revealed how powerful it is when an abuser's behaviour is brought into the open – provided the one who has been abused has control over the disclosure process.

On the other side of the story, we will probably all be familiar with the massive, dreadful, decades-long cover-up of Catholic priests sexually abusing children and women. The church hushed victims and protected abusers, sometimes allowing priests to go on to abuse again and again.

Alas, the Catholic Church is not unique in this. As I write, the Anglican communion is holding an enquiry into historical child sexual abuse. Recently the Southern Baptist denomination in the USA revealed that within their churches pastors and volunteers abused hundreds of women, with over 250 convictions to date.

Holocaust survivor Elie Wiesel famously said, 'I can tolerate the memory of silence, but not the silence of memory.'

* * *

When we silence someone who has been subjected to abuse, we refuse to validate their story. We close down their opportunity to obtain legal justice, restorative justice or therapeutic help.

But bringing things into the light of day has exactly the opposite effect.

Why do churches sometimes silence those who have been abused?

Sometimes it's a theological misunderstanding, as we have seen. Churches believe that they are supporting marriage if they encourage women to return to abusive husbands, to forgive, to submit.

Sometimes it's because the abuser is a prominent person within the church. He might be a powerful figure – the pastor or a wealthy donor. He might just be a plausibly 'nice guy' whom nobody can believe is an abuser. Sometimes it's because the very idea of that 'nice man' being an abuser whom they have failed to identify is very disturbing for a church. Sometimes that's what keeps churches from allowing women to tell.

Sometimes, it's the power of vested interest. Allowing the abuse to come out into the open will bring the church under public scrutiny. It might end up in the papers. It might end up in the courts. And that might 'impede the mission' of the church – as if this were the sort of church that one would want to bring anyone into.

So sometimes churches close ranks. They use various tactics to silence the women. And they promote an impression of 'business as usual'. Women are told to shut up and go home, or they are simply disbelieved. I don't know which of those is more hurtful. Either way, it puts the women right back into harm's way.

But the #MeToo movement was wiser. They knew that these things need to come into the open. And to do that, we must confront the power of vested interest.

Confronting the power of vested interest

> [Jesus and the disciples] went to Capernaum; and when the sabbath came, he entered the synagogue and taught. They were astounded at his teaching, for he taught them as one having authority, and not as the scribes. *Immediately*[64] there was in their synagogue a man with an unclean spirit.
> MARK 1:21–23 (NRSV)

I don't know how well you know the gospel of Mark. It's a pacy, exhilarating account of Jesus' ministry. When I read it, I like to think that I get a sense of that breathless experience of the disciples, trying to keep up with Jesus.

'He did *what*?'
'*Now* where are we going?'

In Mark 1, Jesus' very first action after calling the four disciples Peter, Andrew, James and John is to stride into the synagogue in Capernaum. And immediately they are met with opposition. You'd think it might have taken a few weeks. A few days, anyway. But no, they met immediate resistance.

From whom? Not from grumbling Pharisees or critical scribes, though that would surely come, but on this first occasion, they encounter a demon.

This should disturb us: a demon, in the synagogue? Really? The forces of darkness in the place that should be a bastion for the forces of light? And if this has not disturbed us enough, the creature's words really must:

> 'What have you to do with us, Jesus of Nazareth? Have you come to destroy us? I know who you are, the Holy One of God.'
> v. 24 (NRSV)

What on earth does it mean – 'Have you come to destroy us?' This demon sounds very much like the forces of vested interest and status quo. There is something powerful and rotten at the heart of this synagogue. Something that senses the move of God which is breaking out. Something that smells the change in the wind – and utterly resists it.

Here, at the heart of society, in the urbane city of Capernaum, Jesus has experienced the very first power confrontation of his ministry. He has come up against the powers of darkness, which identify him without doubt as God's emissary and protest his coming. They are only cast down from their strongholds with convulsions and shrieking when he speaks the word of authority. He has met the forces of vested interest and status quo. And they are very powerful indeed.

* * *

One evening, later in his ministry, Jesus was having dinner with a Pharisee. The Pharisees, as you probably know, were super-observant in religious matters and sometimes got their priorities mixed up. Jesus often clashed with them. On this occasion, Jesus attracted criticism for not performing the customary washing of his hands before eating. (This was a religious practice, not a hygiene thing.) In response, he pointed out the hypocrisy of those who were commenting and the confusion of their priorities:

> Woe to you Pharisees, because you give God a tenth of your mint, rue and all other kinds of garden herbs, but you neglect justice and the love of God.
> LUKE 11:42

The Pharisees were good at obeying the letter of the law; they were good at keeping up appearances. But Jesus told them that the most important matters of justice and love were being neglected.

As the evening unfolded, things became more hostile. Another lawyer piled in with questions. Then when Jesus went outside after dinner, he was ambushed by a delegation of scribes and Pharisees who had come to cross-examine him. By then (it's always a good idea to read past the chapter breaks), a crowd had gathered – a large, unruly crowd.

It was then that Jesus made this statement:

> Be on your guard against the yeast of the Pharisees, which is hypocrisy. There is nothing concealed that will not be disclosed, or hidden that will not be made known. What you have said in the dark will be heard in the daylight, and what you have whispered in the ear in the inner rooms will be proclaimed from the roofs.
> LUKE 12:1–3

There is no room for religious hypocrisy or cover-ups in the kingdom of God.

There is nothing hidden that will not be made known

I don't know if you've ever visited a museum which reconstructs houses or cottages from a past age and furnishes them in the style of the period. I grew up in Cardiff, the capital of Wales, and spent many happy afternoons at the wonderful St Fagans National Museum of History just outside the city.

In St Fagans there is a row of tiny miners' cottages, each one decorated in the style of a different era. I remember being fascinated by the lack of a bathroom (until a bath was ingeniously installed in the kitchen in the mid-20th century) and the (to me) quaint decorative styles.

But one thing really sticks in my mind: a picture, probably embroidered, that hung in the family room in the Victorian era and proclaimed, 'Thou, God, seest me.' There, where everyone could see it every day, was the reminder – *you are under divine observation*.

How does such a thought make you feel – comforted or nervous? I sometimes wonder how the psalmist felt when he asked, 'Where can I go from your Spirit? Where can I flee from your presence?' (Psalm 139:7).

If someone is abusing you, then I'd like to suggest that these words might be comforting for you. God sees and knows. What's more, he sees and knows and loves. You have nothing to fear from him.

But for the abuser – those words should make him quake in his boots. God sees. He knows. Nothing is hidden from him.

* * *

We will close this chapter by taking a look at the first half of Psalm 94. It starts like this:

> O Lord, you God of vengeance,
>   you God of vengeance, shine forth!
> Rise up, O judge of the earth;
>   give to the proud what they deserve!
> O Lord, how long shall the wicked,
>   how long shall the wicked exult?
> vv. 1–3 (NRSV)

I don't know how you feel about the idea of vengeance, but it might help to tell you that the word for vengeance would be better translated 'retribution'. It's not about revenge but judicial punishment. This is why the psalmist goes on to ask that the proud (that is, the wicked and haughty) get what they deserve. This is not a prayer for a knife in the back, but for a flashing blue light and a pair of handcuffs.

But take a look at the second stanza. This explains why the psalmist has referred to the wicked as 'proud', because they think they can get away with it:

> They pour out their arrogant words;
>   all the evildoers boast.
> They crush your people, O Lord,
>   and afflict your heritage.
> They kill the widow and the stranger,
>   they murder the orphan,
> and they say, 'The Lord does not see;
>   the God of Jacob does not perceive.'
> vv. 4–7 (NRSV)

Do they imagine that God is too busy to notice? Too preoccupied with great matters? Too sleepy? Too indifferent? Whatever the fantasy they have constructed for themselves, they have made a horrible miscalculation:

Understand, O dullest of the people;
    fools, when will you be wise?
He who planted the ear, does he not hear?
He who formed the eye, does he not see?
He who disciplines the nations,
he who teaches knowledge to humankind,
    does he not chastise?

vv. 8–10 (NRSV)

God sees.

Oh, he sees.

And everything that has been said and done in the dark will be heard
and seen in the light of God's truth.

III

THREE PERSONAL ADDRESSES

10

To those trapped by an abuser

This whole book has been addressed to you, so I will add very little here.

I hope that it has been helpful to you. I hope that it has brought you life and hope.

My prayer is that it has helped you to understand your worth and value before God and his utter, implacable commitment to your freedom and well-being, and the freedom and well-being of all who have been abused. My prayer is that it has helped to unlock some of the chains that may be keeping you in harm's way and that you are now confident that there is nothing in the Bible that tells you that you must put up with it.

'A Christian wife's duty is to submit to abuse': does the Bible tell me this? Absolutely not.

* * *

If after reading this book you feel that you are ready to move forward and perhaps even take steps to leave your husband, it is important to carefully plan this and think it through. You will likely know what is and isn't safe for you, so do listen to and trust yourself and your instincts. It's important to know that you could be in more danger if you don't plan ahead. I'm not the person to advise you on this in detail, though. So in these concluding words I want to signpost you to some places which might be able to help you.

There is a 'Further reading' section on page 163, which suggests some titles that you might like to follow up on. In particular, I'd like to highlight to you the resource produced by Restored, which is free to anyone who has been subjected to abuse. I'd also like to highlight Natalie Collins' excellent book *Out of Control*, which contains an extensive selection of resources at the back.

On page 166 is a Safety Plan which it would be wise to fill out, whether or not you are currently intending to leave your partner. The 'Taking it further' section on page 163 also contains helplines, blogs and websites that might help.

In an emergency, dial 999.

11

To church leaders

In chapter 4 we discussed the way that churches sometimes urge women to forgive the abuser far too quickly and readily. In chapter 9 we considered the dangers of silence and the way that churches sometimes close ranks to protect themselves or powerful people within the church. If you have skipped directly to this part of the book, I encourage you to go back and read the whole thing, but particularly those two chapters.

In this chapter I would like to make a few other concluding remarks to urge you to do everything in your power to keep women and children safe and to foster a culture of safety for everyone in your congregation.

Believe the woman!

I have lost count of how many stories I have heard and read of churches failing to support women in their congregation who disclose that their husband is abusive.

> After 14 years of abuse, I was told by my priest, 'It's a storm in a teacup.'
>
> After pouring out my heart (it took a long time to summon the courage), the vicar blamed me for the abuse.
>
> The instinct of male ministers seems to be to confront the perpetrator ('Come on, old chap, behave a bit better won't you?'), which prompts a public denial ('She's just a silly little

woman…') and a private victimisation ('What have you been saying to the pastor, you stupid woman?').

Witness statements in In Churches Too: Church responses to domestic abuse – a case study in Cumbria (2018)

Sometimes this is because domestic abuse is misdiagnosed as a relationship issue, one that requires marital counselling. There is a world of difference between a couple who are having marital difficulties and one whose power imbalance is abusive.

Sometimes this is because abusers lie so plausibly, and in particular because they very effectively employ the strategy Deny, Attack, Reverse Victim and Offender (DARVO).[65]

Sometimes the church's reluctance to support the woman relates to allowing the husband a presumption of innocence.

In law in most countries (and under the UN Declaration of Human Rights), a person is considered innocent until they are proven guilty. But this presumption of innocence is a juridical stance. It never prevents (for example) the police from detaining someone they believe to have committed violent actions, pending trial. The police act in the interests of the public who might be harmed, until the person is found guilty or not guilty. And in the same way, the legal presumption of innocence should never prevent a church from taking action to help a woman find a place of safety.

After serious allegations have been made, presumption of the husband's innocence within the church context is very problematic, for at least three reasons. First, because – to put it rather simplistically – if the husband is innocent, the wife must be guilty of lying. Presumption of the man's innocence is a presumption of the woman's guilt. British newspaper *The Independent* put this neatly in a recent article about allegations of sexual assault:

- ✸ The presumption of innocence has become problematic in its wider usage *outside* the courtroom... In championing the presumption of innocence for the defendant, there's a tendency to descend upon the complainant, and try to destroy their character and credibility. Instead, our immediate reaction when alleged victims do come forward should not be to question their reliability, but to listen.[66]

✸ A second reason for taking the woman's testimony seriously is because failure to do so will make others much less likely to seek the help that they need.

Third, and most pressingly, the harm that might come to the wife through believing the husband far exceeds the harm that might come to the husband through believing the wife. Yes, of course the slurring of someone's name is damaging, if it turns out to be untrue. But that is what the legal process is designed to test. It is not the church's responsibility to test that. By contrast, though, the consequences for disbelieving a woman who has disclosed domestic abuse can be fatal.

This would be in line with standard church operating procedures for the safeguarding of adults at risk. For example, the 'Safe to Belong' policy of my own, UK Baptist, church family states:

It is important to act if you suspect abuse – don't wait until you are absolutely sure. This doesn't mean that you are jumping to conclusions or making judgements about the situation, it simply means that there is a safeguarding concern.[67]

Believe women. Keep them, and any children, safe. Report allegations of criminal behaviour to the police and cooperate with the ensuing process. Signpost women to their local domestic abuse services. If there are children in the home, you must report concerns to the local safeguarding team.

Then you can start to think about how to offer pastoral support to everyone who is affected by the situation. It can be tempting to try to help a couple reconcile, but this is often not appropriate and in fact couple counselling is contraindicated. It puts the relationship in the category of dysfunctional marriage, with the implication that both partners just need to try a bit harder, rather than into the category of criminal activity. Once again, there is a world of difference between a couple who are having marital difficulties and a relationship where one partner is abusing the other. Couple counselling for the latter is likely to prolong the abuse.[68]

Exercise church discipline

We looked earlier at Jesus' words in Matthew 18, which show a three-stage process for repeat offenders in the church:

> If your brother or sister sins, go and point out their fault, just between the two of you. If they listen to you, you have won them over. But if they will not listen, take one or two others along, so that 'every matter may be established by the testimony of two or three witnesses.' If they still refuse to listen, tell it to the church; and if they refuse to listen even to the church, treat them as you would a pagan or a tax collector.
>
> MATTHEW 18:15–17

On average, domestic abuse victims have suffered for 2.7 years and experienced 50 abuse events before they manage to report it to someone who will listen.[69] That means that they have more than satisfied Jesus' first step of pointing out the fault privately, and it is more than time to move to step two or three. It also means that they have more than satisfied the criteria of turning the other cheek.

Note that Jesus simply assumes that the offence will be taken seriously by the church. There is no question about that.

Your church or denomination will probably have established procedures for church discipline. As you know, Jesus isn't asking us to anathematise the offender; he is calling us to exclude them for the sake that they might be won back into faith (as he expects us to aim to win unbelievers). Paul appears to be following very much this line in 1 Corinthians 5:1–5 and – presuming this refers to the same case – 2 Corinthians 2:5–11.

Again, it is clear that both Jesus and Paul expect us to take offences of this nature extremely seriously. There is no 'ignore it' clause.

And do, please, think very carefully about whether an abuser can safely attend the same church as his victim, even if he professes to be repentant (and not all repentance is genuine). There will almost certainly be another church in town where he can receive pastoral care and where he can worship without re-traumatising his wife or ex-wife every week.

What culture are you cultivating? Is it facilitating the abuser or the victim? Are you balancing your messages about forgiveness and sin with messages about God's heart for the oppressed and downtrodden?

Call out sin

Call horrible, 'horrible'.

Abuse survivor, interview transcript

One of the abiding messages for me in the prophecy of Jeremiah is his scathing attack on the false prophets who were ignoring the threat of the Babylonian incursion and making smooth promises to the people that all was well when it patently was not:

> They dress the wound of my people
>   as though it were not serious.

'Peace, peace,' they say,
>   when there is no peace.

JEREMIAH 6:14

Biblical scholar Walter Brueggemann tells us that the first step towards prophetic obedience is the naming of what is wrong: a commitment to truth-telling that overcomes indolence, indifference and vested interest.

I venture to suggest that the prophetic task of the preacher and the duty of the pastoral leader is to tell the truth, to call what is horrible, 'horrible', and to do so boldly, even when what is horrible is to be found within our own church.

Sometimes that will be costly in terms of our church reputation, our congregation numbers (and hence finance) and even perhaps our own personal reputation. But we dare not put ourselves on the wrong side of Jesus' warnings:

Woe to you who laugh now,
>   for you will mourn and weep.

LUKE 6:25

If any of you put a stumbling-block before one of these little ones who believe in me, it would be better for you if a great millstone were fastened around your neck and you were drowned in the depth of the sea. Woe to the world because of stumbling-blocks! Occasions for stumbling are bound to come, but woe to the one by whom the stumbling-block comes!

MATTHEW 18:6–7 (NRSV)

Nor, indeed, can we afford to ignore the words of Ezekiel to the religious leaders of Israel, or of James to leaders in the church:

Woe to you shepherds of Israel who only take care of yourselves! Should not shepherds take care of the flock?

EZEKIEL 34:2

> Not many of you should become teachers, my fellow believers, because you know that we who teach will be judged more strictly.
>
> JAMES 3:1

Establish cultures where women can truly flourish

If you lead a church with complementarian theology, I hope that you feel I have been fair to your position, and that I have shown that your position does not inherently validate domestic abuse. But what I would like to say to you, in closing, is this: please take care! Because your church system is inherently more dangerous in terms of domestic abuse than a church with egalitarian theology.

Please hear me well. I'm not accusing you of intentional complicity with abusers or of leading an abusive church. But I am saying that your theological position is more open to abusive misinterpretation. This is because there can be significant overlap between complementarian theology and the sort of masculine hegemony that supports abuse.

Please let me explain.

A hegemony is a system of inequality that is sustained by ideas rather than by force.[70] As Raewyn Connell puts it:

> It means ascendancy achieved within a balance of forces, that is, a state of play. Other patterns and groups are subordinated rather than eliminated.[71]

So a theological idea, such as male headship or female submission, can function to establish or sustain a balance of forces that entraps women – a subordination or marginalisation of the female voice and the female perspective.

In a complementarian church, there is a real possibility of finding some or all of the following characteristics of male hegemony: a power imbalance between men and women; a sense of entitlement by men; a perception that men's ministry is of more value than women's (and hence that men are more valuable than women); the subordination of women's will to men's; and punishment of women who transgress established gender roles (for example, by means of church discipline or ostracism).

The presence of any of these within your church is a red-flag sign that it is hegemonic; and masculine hegemony is conducive to sexual and domestic violence.

Are there such elements within your church? Dare I suggest that you might not presume to know the answer to this question, but should ask some of the women you serve?

The onus is on you to ensure that your theology can *never* be used as a means of grooming women to submit to an abuser; that it can *never* be misunderstood as promoting a hegemonic masculinity; and that women are actively encouraged to report abuse. Inaction is not enough. You will need to actively seek out dangerous misinterpretations of your teaching and correct them.

Many, many experiences show that it's not enough to protest, when challenged, that the silencing or subordination of women is not what God desires (in other words, that your theology is pure). Nor is it enough to assert, when challenged, that this is not what you intended in your church (that your preaching is godly). If you aren't actively, vigorously and continually counteracting the dangers of male hegemony, there is a very real possibility that you are or will become complicit in abuse.

Please take this seriously. Because women's blood is crying out from the ground for justice.

12

To the perpetrator

And finally, a note to abusers.

If you've picked this up and read this far, then maybe you have been convicted of your need to change. Most abusers don't set out to be bad people, and many have moments when they aspire to live a better way. If this is such a moment for you, *you need to act now*. Good intentions will not do. You need to take concrete steps to ensure that this never, ever happens again.

Repentance – let's call it by its proper name – is not easy, and it takes humility and determination. Moments when we have a soft heart do not last if we ignore them. If you make excuses, put it off for another day or just allow the process of time to take away the sense of urgency, nothing will change. You will continue to abuse; you will continue to cause harm to people you claim to love.

You may remember the words of Jesus from the sermon on the mount:

> If your right eye causes you to stumble, gouge it out and throw it away. It is better for you to lose one part of your body than for your whole body to be thrown into hell. And if your right hand causes you to stumble, cut it off and throw it away. It is better for you to lose one part of your body than for your whole body to go into hell.
>
> MATTHEW 5:29–30

Repentance may be very costly for you. You will have to admit you have done dreadful things – admit it not just to yourself and the person you are abusing, but to other people and to God. You will have to seek to make restitution for what you have done – and restitution will not be on your terms. Your wife may end the relationship – and you will have no say in that. You may have to surrender yourself to criminal prosecution. Repentance will require you to cooperate fully with that process. But as you weigh your choices, know this: *the Bible gives you no support for what you do. And God is firmly, implacably, on the side of the vulnerable and the abused.* Those who abuse others find themselves pitched in opposition to God – and that is a dreadful place to be.

But know this, too:

> If we confess our sins, he is faithful and just and will forgive us our sins and purify us from all unrighteousness.
> 1 JOHN 1:9

There is forgiveness – even for you. Extraordinarily, God loves abusers, as well as those they abuse. The death of Jesus is sufficient for your sin – yes, even yours. The grace of God is sufficient for your forgiveness – yes, even yours. And your heavenly Father waits with his arms outstretched for his son to come home confessing, 'Father, I have sinned against heaven and against you. I am no longer worthy to be called your son' (Luke 15:21). And when you repent there will be great celebration:

> There will be more rejoicing in heaven over one sinner who repents than over ninety-nine righteous people who do not need to repent.
> LUKE 15:7

Do it. Just do it. For the sake of those you abuse, and for the sake of your soul.

* * *

And if you are going to do it, you need help. There is expert, professional help that you can access. There is a phone line you can ring, and you will be put in touch with perpetrator programmes in your area. If you want to change, this is the first thing you can do. Turn to the 'Taking it further' section on the next page for more information.

May God give you the strength to begin a new way today.

Taking it further

General further reading

Church of England, *Responding Well to Domestic Abuse: Policy and practice guidance* (Church of England, 2017), **churchofengland. org/sites/default/files/2017-11/responding-well-to-domestic-abuse-formatted-master-copy-030317.pdf**.

Natalie Collins, *Out of Control: Couples, conflict and the capacity for change* (SPCK, 2019).

Nikki Dhillon-Keane, *Domestic Abuse in Church Communities: A safe pastoral response* (Redemptorist, 2018).

Lisa Oakley and Justin Humphreys, *Escaping the Maze of Spiritual Abuse: Creating healthy Christian cultures* (SPCK, 2019).

Lucy Peppiatt, *Rediscovering Scripture's Vision for Women: Fresh perspectives on disputed texts* (InterVarsity Press, 2019).

Esther Sweetman (ed.), *Restored: A handbook for female Christian survivors of domestic abuse* (Restored, 2019). This is free to any survivor of domestic abuse (subject to availability). See **restoredrelationships.org**.

Ruth Tucker, *Black and White Bible, Black and Blue Wife: My story of finding hope after domestic abuse* (Zondervan, 2016).

Helplines and support organisations for victims and those who support them

In an emergency, ring 999.

National Domestic Abuse Helpline

If you have been personally affected by abuse or violence or are still with an abusive or violent partner, you can get help. If you are based in the UK, you can call the National Domestic Abuse Helpline. It's a confidential 24-hour service.

Website: **nationaldahelpline.org.uk**
Tel: **Freephone 0808 2000 247**

Women's Aid

A national organisation which provides advice, support and a 24-hour abuse helpline.

Website: **womensaid.org.uk**

Refuge

Offers support, in partnership with Women's Aid, to help women and children escaping domestic violence.

Website: **refuge.org.uk**
Email: **info@refuge.org.uk**

Local domestic abuse services

There will be an organisation local to you that can support you. However, it can be hard to find on the internet. The most reliable method is to put the name of your local council *and* the words 'domestic abuse' into a search engine.

Resources for churches

Church of England, *Responding Well to Domestic Abuse: Policy and practice guidance* (Church of England, 2017), **churchofengland.org/sites/default/files/2017-11/responding-well-to-domestic-abuse-formatted-master-copy-030317.pdf**.

Nikki Dhillon-Keane, *Domestic Abuse in Church Communities: A safe pastoral response* (Redemptorist, 2018).

Restored, *Ending Domestic Abuse: A pack for churches* **restoredrelationships.org/resources/info/51**.

Restored, *DARVO: Deny, Attack, Reverse Victim and Offender* **restoredrelationships.org/news/2017/11/07/darvo-deny-attack-reverse-victim-and-offender**.

And this very helpful resource produced by and for the Australian church: **saferresource.org.au**.

Resource for abusers

Respect

Confidential helpline offering advice, information and support to help you stop being violent and abusive to your partner.

Freephone 0808 802 4040 Monday–Friday 9.00 am–5.00 pm.
Email: **info@respectphoneline.org.uk**

Blogs

If you want to think more about issues discussed in the book, here are some blogs that might help you:

confusiontoclaritynow.com
flyingfreenow.com
unholycharade.com/resources

Safety plan[72]

Some women leave the home they share with the abusive partner. These are protective actions you may wish to consider if you are in this situation. Even if you are not planning to leave your partner, it is important to review a safety plan regarding leaving in case the violence escalates and you need to leave quickly.

1 It may not be safe to inform my partner that I am leaving.

2 Should I need to leave quickly, it would be helpful for me to leave some emergency cash, an extra set of house and car keys and extra clothes with some people who I can go to for help.

3 I can keep copies of important documentation such as immigration papers or birth certificates at someone's house.

4 I can open a savings account to increase my freedom to leave. I should make sure to alert the bank not to send any correspondence to my home address.

5 I can get legal advice from a solicitor who understands domestic abuse. But, as with the bank, I should make certain the solicitor knows not to send any correspondence to my home address. (It is critical to consult with a family solicitor if you have any children. Your local domestic abuse service may be able to recommend a suitable solicitor.)

6 The local domestic abuse helpline number is .... I can seek safe shelter and support by calling this helpline.

7 I can keep change for phone calls on me at all times. I must be careful if I am using my mobile or home number because my partner or ex could see the numbers I have called on next month's telephone bill. To keep telephone communications confidential, I can use a pay phone, a friend's phone or a pay-as-you-go mobile phone that my partner or ex is unaware of.

8 These are people that I could ask for assistance with:

a Money ....

b Childcare ....

c Support attending appointments
....

d Transportation ....

e Other ....

9 If I need to return home to get personal belongings, I can call the police for an escort to stand by and keep the peace. To do this, I call 999 and ask the police to meet me somewhere close to my home. They will stay while I pick up my personal belongings and those of my children.

10 Other protective actions I have considered are:

....

....

....

....

....

....

....

....

When leaving an abusive partner, it is important I take certain items with me. Items with asterisks on the following list are the most important, but if there is time the other items might be taken, or stored outside the house. Keeping them all together in one location makes it much easier if I need to leave in a hurry.

a   Identification for myself*
b   Children's birth certificates*
c   Any papers relating to injunctions or other legal proceedings*
d   My birth certificate*
e   Immigration papers*
f   School and vaccination records*
g   Money*
h   Cheque book, bank book/cards*
i   Credit cards*
j   Keys – house/car/office*
k   Driver's licence and car ownership details*
l   Medication*
m   Passport(s)*
n   Any medical records*
o   Divorce/separation papers*
p   House lease/mortgage/insurance documents*
q   Address book*
r   Pictures/photos
s   Children's favourite toys/blankets
t   Jewellery
u   Items of special sentimental value

11 Telephone numbers I need to know (for safety reasons I may need to keep these telephone numbers hidden (but accessible!) and/or memorise them):

   a Police ....

   b Domestic Abuse helpline (24 hours) ....

       ....

   c Solicitor ....

   d Work ....

   e Religious leader ....

   f Other ....

Notes

1 The #SheToo podcast series can be found at **biblesociety.org.uk/explore-the-bible/shetoo**.

2 **gov.uk/government/publications/domestic-abuse-recognise-the-signs/domestic-abuse-recognise-the-signs#how-to-recognise-domestic-abuse-in-a-relationship**

3 See, for example, Leonie Westenberg, '"When she calls for help": domestic violence in Christian families', *Social Sciences* 6:3 (2017), p. 71.

4 A. Myhill, 'Measuring coercive control: what can we learn from national population surveys?' *Violence Against Women*, 21:3 (2015), pp. 355–75.

5 **ons.gov.uk/peoplepopulationandcommunity/crimeandjustice/bulletins/domesticabuseinenglandandwales/yearendingmarch2018**

6 The Colossians passage is very similar, and I won't deal with it separately.

7 See Daniel B. Wallace, *Greek Grammar beyond the Basics: An exegetical syntax of the New Testament* (Harper Collins, 1996), p. 651; also discussion on the middle voice on pp. 414–30.

8 Ben Witherington III, *The Letters to Philemon, the Colossians, and the Ephesians: A socio-rhetorical commentary on the captivity epistles* (Eerdmans, 2007), p. 190.

9 Ruth Tucker, *Black and White Bible, Black and Blue Wife: My story of finding hope after domestic abuse* (Zondervan, 2016), p. 47.

10 Andrew T. Lincoln, *Ephesians*, Word Biblical Commentary Vol. 42 (Word, 1990), p. 364.

11 Jacob Neusner, *The Mishnah: A new translation* (Yale University Press, 1988), p. 389. Ketubot 4:5; 5:5, 7; 6:1; 7:6, 8.

12 William J. Webb, *Slaves, Women and Homosexuals: Exploring the hermeneutics of cultural analysis* (InterVarsity Press, 2001), p. 32.

13 Tucker, *Black and White Bible, Black and Blue Wife*, p. 77.

14 George W. Knight III, 'Husbands and wives as analogues of Christ and the church: Ephesians 5:21–33 and Colossians 3:18–19', in John Piper and Wayne Grudem (eds), *Recovering Biblical Manhood and Womanhood: A response to evangelical feminism* (Crossway, 1991), p. 171.

15   Tucker, *Black and White Bible, Black and Blue Wife*, p. 190.

16   I am aware that the authorship of the Petrine epistles is disputed. However, it is easier to refer to the author as 'Peter', as the epistle does, whatever his actual identity.

17   Steve Carter, 'A charter for domestic violence? The subordination of slaves and wives in 1 Peter' in Helen Paynter and Michael Spalione (eds), *The Bible on Violence: A thick description* (Sheffield Phoenix, 2020), pp. 168–190.

18   Gilbert Bilezikian, *Beyond Sex Roles: What the Bible says about a woman's place in church and family*, third edition (Baker Academic, 2006), p. 146.

19   It is deeply regrettable that it took until 1991 before the law in England and Wales recognised that a woman did not give her husband, upon marriage, 'implied consent' to intercourse under all circumstances.

20   Michael Gorman, *Cruciformity: Paul's narrative spirituality of the cross* (Eerdmans, 2001).

21   **reviveourhearts.com/true-woman/manifesto/read**

22   Quoted in Carolyn Corretti and Sukumar P. Desai, 'The legacy of Eve's curse: religion, childbirth pain, and the rise of anesthesia in Europe: c. 1200–1800s', *Journal of Anesthesia History* 4 (2018), pp. 182–90.

23   Tucker, *Black and White Bible, Black and Blue Wife*, pp. 43–44.

24   Both of these quotations formed part of *Eva's Call*, a community piece of artwork done by ordinands and staff at Cuddesdon College in 2018. It can be seen at **artsrcc.wordpress.com/2018/03/02/evas-call**.

25   Scot McKnight, *Galatians*, NIV Application Commentary (Zondervan, 1995), p. 120.

26   Don Carson, '"Silent in the churches": on the role of women in 1 Corinthians 14:33b–36', in Piper and Grudem, *Recovering Biblical Manhood and Womanhood*, p. 153.

27   Tom Wright, *1 Corinthians*, Paul for Everyone (SPCK, 2003), pp. 198–200.

28   Kirk MacGregor, '1 Corinthians 14:33b–38 as a Pauline quotation-refutation device', *Priscilla Papers* 32(1) (2018), pp. 23–28.

29   Gordon D. Fee, *The First Epistle to the Corinthians*, New International Commentary on the New Testament (Eerdmans, 1987), pp. 697–708.

30   Richard Clark Kroeger and Catherine Clark Kroeger, *I Suffer Not a Woman: Rethinking 1 Timothy 2:11–15 in light of ancient evidence* (Baker Academic, 1998).

31   Kroeger and Kroeger, *I Suffer Not a Woman*, p. 11.

32   Knight III, 'Husbands and wives as analogues of Christ and the church', p. 169.

33   Council for Biblical Manhood and Womanhood, Nashville Statement (2017), article 3, **cbmw.org/nashville-statement**.

34   See Exodus 21:10–11. Notice that the language here is of the wife 'going out', not of 'sending out', which is what is expressed in Malachi.

35   David Instone-Brewer, *Divorce and Remarriage in the Bible: The social and literary context* (Eerdmans, 2002), p. 57. My emphasis.

36   Instone-Brewer, *Divorce and Remarriage in the Bible*, pp. 110–14.

37   'Truly I tell you, until heaven and earth pass away, not one letter, not one stroke of a letter, will pass from the law until all is accomplished. Therefore, whoever breaks one of the least of these commandments, and teaches others to do the same, will be called least in the kingdom of heaven' (Matthew 5:18–19, NRSV).

38   Translation is Dr Grudem's own.

39   See **waynegrudem.com/grounds-for-divorce-why-i-now-believe-there-are-more-than-two**

40   W.M. Foley, 'Marriage (Christian)' in W.H.R. Rivers et al. (eds), *Encyclopaedia of Religion and Ethics*, Volume 8 (T & T Clark, 1908–1926), p. 438.

41   Presbyterians Against Domestic Violence Network, 'Remembering victims of domestic violence and abuse remembrance: where healing begins', **presbyterianmission.org/wp-content/uploads/domestic-violence-worship-resources.pdf**.

42   See Miroslav Volf, *Free of Charge: Giving and forgiving in a culture stripped of grace* (Zondervan, 2005), and *Exclusion and Embrace: A theological exploration of identity, otherness, and reconciliation* (Abingdon, 1996).

43   Volf, *Free of Charge*, p. 140.

44   Volf, *Free of Charge*, p. 153.

45   Walter Wink, *Jesus and Nonviolence: A third way* (Fortress Press, 2003), p. 16.

46   I accept that the authorship of some of these epistles is disputed, but I have chosen to go with the traditional readings. In any case, most of the prominent members of the early church faced persecution and many faced martyrdom, so the point is valid even if the authors are not as I have suggested.

47   I have written about how Christians can use the psalms that pray for

violence against the enemy in my book *God of Violence Yesterday, God of Love Today? Wrestling honestly with the Old Testament* (BRF, 2019).

48   Here the NIV's 'a man like myself' has been substituted with the NRSV's more gender-inclusive language 'my equal'.

49   Quoted in Lesley Orr Macdonald, *Out of the Shadows: Christianity and violence against women in Scotland* (Centre for Theology and Public Issues, 2001), p. 20.

50   This is not to say that abuse doesn't happen in Baptist churches, sadly. But maybe our particular church set-up lends itself a little less to abuse by those in power than some others.

51   Some would argue that David's actions amounted to rape.

52   Quoted in Macdonald, *Out of the Shadows*, p. 20.

53   Tom Wright, *Matthew for Everyone, Part 2: Chapters 16–28* (SPCK, 2004), p. 31.

54   The Bechdel test is a test applied to modern fiction, particularly films. It asks if the work features at least two women who talk to each other about something other than a man.

55   Here I am drawing on the work of Scott Nikaido, 'Hagar and Ishmael as literary figures: an intertextual study', *Vetus Testamentum* 51:2 (2001), pp. 219–42.

56   Quoted in Macdonald, *Out of the Shadows*, p. 20.

57   David Tombs and Rocío Figueroa Alvear, *Recognising Jesus as a Victim of Sexual Abuse: Responses from Sodalicio survivors in Peru* (Centre for Theology and Public Issues, University of Otago, 2019), p. 4.

58   Dorothy L. Sayers, 'The human-not-quite-human', in *Are Women Human? Penetrating, sensible and witty essays on the role of women in society* (Eerdmans, 2005), p. 68.

59   'Caring Well: A report from the SBC Sexual Abuse Advisory Group', 2019, p. 4, **caringwell.com/wp-content/uploads/2019/06/ SBC-Caring-Well-Report-June-2019.pdf**.

60   Quoted in Macdonald, *Out of the Shadows*, p. 20.

61   Natalie Collins, *Out of Control: Couples, conflict and the capacity for change* (SPCK, 2019), p. 34.

62   Lucy Peppiatt, *Rediscovering Scripture's Vision for Women: Fresh perspectives on disputed texts* (InterVarsity Press, 2019), p. 22.

63   Corrie ten Boom, *Tramp for the Lord* (Christian Literature Crusade, 1974), p. 55.

64   I have replaced 'Just then' in the NRSV with the more literal 'Immediately'.

65 restoredrelationships.org/news/2017/11/07/darvo-deny-attack-reverse-victim-and-offender

66 Malvika Jaganmohan, 'The presumption of innocence is essential – but it should never mean presuming the guilt of the accuser', *The Independent*, 6 January 2015, **independent.co.uk/voices/comment/the-presumption-of-innocence-is-at-the-core-of-our-legal-system-but-we-need-to-rethink-our-approach-9960234.html**

67 The Baptist Union of Great Britain, *Safe to Belong: Safeguarding adults at risk policy* (Baptist Union of Great Britain, 2015), p. 15, **baptist.org.uk/Articles/450987/Safe_to_Belong.aspx**

68 Church of England, *Responding Well to Domestic Abuse* (Church of England, 2017), **churchofengland.org/sites/default/files/2017-11/responding-well-to-domestic-abuse-formatted-master-copy-030317.pdf**, p. 16.

69 safelives.org.uk/policy-evidence/about-domestic-abuse/how-long-do-people-live-domestic-abuse-and-when-do-they-get

70 Thomas R. Bates, 'Gramsci and the theory of hegemony', *Journal of the History of Ideas* (1975), pp. 351–66.

71 Raewyn W. Connell, *Gender and Power: Society, the person and sexual politics* (University of California Press, 1987), p. 184.

72 This safety plan is reproduced, with kind permission of the publisher and the author, from Collins, *Out of Control*, pp. 270–73.

Do you find the violence in the Old Testament a problem? Does it get in the way of reading the Bible – and of faith itself? While acknowledging that there are no easy answers, in *God of Violence Yesterday, God of Love Today?*, Helen Paynter faces the tough questions head-on and offers a fresh, accessible approach to a significant issue. For all those seeking to engage with the Bible and gain confidence in the God it portrays, she provides tools for reading and interpreting biblical texts, and points to ways of dealing with the overall trajectories of violence.

God of Violence Yesterday, God of Love Today?
Wrestling honestly with the Old Testament
Helen Paynter
978 0 85746 639 6 £9.99

brfonline.org.uk

Enabling all ages to grow in faith

Anna Chaplaincy
Living Faith
Messy Church
Parenting for Faith

The Bible Reading Fellowship (BRF) is a Christian charity that resources individuals and churches. Our vision is to enable people of all ages to grow in faith and understanding of the Bible and to see more people equipped to exercise their gifts in leadership and ministry.

To find out more about our ministries and programmes, visit
brf.org.uk